D1398167

DO·IT·YOURSELF
INDOOR PROJECTS

Sterling Publishing Co., Inc.   New York

Published by
Sterling Publishing Co, Inc.
Two Park Avenue, New York,
N.Y. 10016

This book may not be sold outside the
United States of America and Canada

© Marshall Cavendish Limited 1988

ISBN 0–8069–6947–4

Typeset by J&L Composition Ltd, Filey,
North Yorkshire, England

Printed and bound in Hong Kong

This material was previously published in the
Marshall Cavendish partwork *Do It Right*.

Picture credits

John Badminton: 80–84.
Dave King: 9–13, 18–21, 30–32, 52–55, 64, 69, 70.
Steve Lyne: 14, 26, 34–37, 65–67, 85–89,
    108–111.
Ranald MacKechnie: 68, 94–98.
Alan Marsh: 15–17, 22–25, 38–41, 48–51, 56–59,
    72–75, 90–93.
W.H. Newson: 47(b)
Gareth Trevor: 42–47, 76–79, 99–107.

▲ CONTENTS

▲ INTRODUCTION

Constructing your own furniture is a sure way of obtaining exactly what you want, to fit exactly where you want it, and at a fraction of the price of a ready-made item. It is also a pleasurable pastime. The projects in this book have been carefully designed, and many alternative design ideas are included to help you adapt them to your own requirements.

The first nine projects are built-in, starting with the common situation of wanting to fit units into an alcove. Built-in units have the advantage that the building acts as the supporting structure, thereby simplifying the construction. There then follows a selection of freestanding projects, the first of which is a sturdy workbench – a good starting point if you don't already possess one. Many of the projects are designed with storage in mind – remember to plan for the future as storage requirements have a habit of increasing.

Each project is accompanied by a checklist of the tools and materials that you will need to complete it, so you should not find part of the way through the job, that you are missing some vital item. A list of optional items is also included.

Much of the satisfaction of woodworking is measured by the quality of the end result. Cross-references are given in each project to the relevant pages in the Skills Guide at the end of the book so, if you are uncertain about any of the techniques involved, you can refer to them. Read through the instructions for the project from start to finish before starting work so you have overall picture of what is involved in its construction.

Buying good quality materials and know-ing the faults to avoid when buying them is essential to achieve a constructed project you are proud of. Nominal and actual wood sizes vary, so it is important to check the actual sizes of the wood you are using before working out a cutting list. Any number of elaborate and expensive tools will not create good workmanship. Knowing how to use them, however, is another secret of success. You will also find information on how to set out the parts accurately using the correct methods and equipment. Always remember to check and double check all dimensions before proceeding – a pencil line is easy to erase and reposition, but undersized pieces of wood are costly and cause frustration. A good carpenter will only use a cutting list as a guide – at each stage of the construction, the dimensions of the parts being cut to size should be measured to fit exactly.

Finally, a few notes on safety. Read manufacturers' instructions carefully before using equipment with which you are not familiar. Remember, when attaching a unit to a wall, to check first for concealed pipes and wiring; small electronic detectors are available which make this task easy, but a general rule is never to make attachments vertically above or below electrical fittings and to avoid the vicinity of pipe runs near plumbing appliances. Avoid wearing loose clothing when using power tools as it can become entangled and cause serious injury. Always unplug power tools before making any adjustments. Finally, allow yourself plenty of time to complete the job so as to insure that the end result is of the high quality that you deserve and will enjoy using.

MIKE TRIER

Built-in Alcove Unit

An empty alcove is an open invitation for a made-to-measure display cabinet; built-in furniture makes the best use of space. This design offers a foolproof way to fit a fully adaptable feature cabinet.

An alcove cries out for a fitted storage and display cabinet – a chimney recess is invariably the focal point for a room and an excellent place to put your TV, hi-fi set and assorted ornaments and plants. But there are other advantages to a made-to-measure cabinet that's adapted to fit your recess and to accommodate the things you want.

Free-standing storage furniture requires a high degree of woodworking skill to insure that it's rigid and stable. Even then it's bound to waste some space at the sides. An alcove unit doesn't – the recess walls form a reliable anchor and reduce the amount of material (and skill) you'll need. The only difficulty is that the walls of the alcove may be out-of-square.

Side uprights form flat and level surfaces on which to mount the shelves so, once they're up, you can depend on everything being square and half your problems being over.

Veneered chipboard shelves solve the rest. They're available in a variety of widths and require very little finishing – you'll only need to cut them to length to make abutting pieces match in size and color.

The assembly line that follows is suitable for alcoves wider than 5ft and 16in deep but there's no end to the adaptations you can make to fit out your alcove. If in doubt about fitting the fluorescent light, contact a qualified electrician.

DESIGN FOR AN ALCOVE UNIT

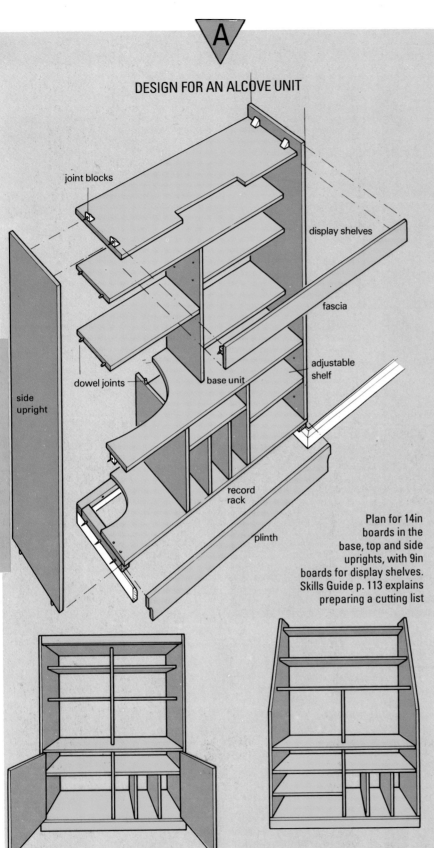

joint blocks

display shelves

fascia

dowel joints

base unit

adjustable shelf

side upright

record rack

plinth

Plan for 14in boards in the base, top and side uprights, with 9in boards for display shelves. Skills Guide p. 113 explains preparing a cutting list

Narrow alcoves – less than 4ft wide – may need no vertical base dividers. Shelves can be strengthened with blocks.

The base unit can be divided to accommodate only hi-fi equipment and ornaments. Dividers in the base unit give the top more strength.

FIT THE BASE AND PLINTH

Screw cleats level on all three sides. Allow for the plinth at the front

An accurate base is essential as the starting point for the unit, which should be no deeper than 14 in. A power outlet can power TV, hi-fi equipment or a light fixture

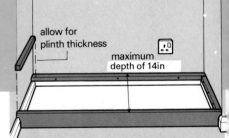

allow for plinth thickness

maximum depth of 14in

Cut a board to fit from floor to the top of the cleat, cut it to fit and add joint blocks

Erect a firm and absolutely level base support. Screw cleats to the walls, allowing ⅝in at the front to accept the plinth. Cut and scribe a plinth to fit level.

SCRIBE AND FIT BASE

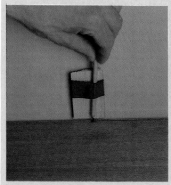

If the back wall is uneven, mark the back edge to fit the contour

insert dowels for side uprights

screw to wall cleats

Lift out the base, then shape with a surform plane

Cut a base and scribe it to fit along its back edge. It must be level on top and flush with, or proud of, the front. Mark and drill dowel holes on the ends of the uprights and matching holes at the sides of the base.

ATTACH THE SIDE UPRIGHTS

If you are fitting a light, conceal the cord behind a bevelled edge on the side panel

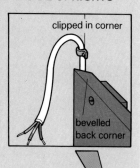

clipped in corner

bevelled back corner

light cord

dowel joints to keep square

Pack gaps behind side panels to make them truly upright

Dowel joint the uprights to the base, then check for level. You may need to scribe the back edges for a really neat fit. If you are fitting a light at the top, accommodate cord at this stage by bevelling the back corner.

ATTACH THE TOP AND FASCIA

Use a coping saw to make a cutout for a light in the top deck

joint blocks   cutout for light

fascia

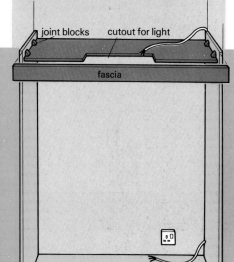

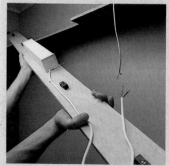

Attach the fascia with joint blocks. Link up the light cord

The top should fit neatly between the uprights – they should be the same distance apart for the full height. Cut the top to accommodate the fascia and, if you wish, to fit the light. Use joint blocks to attach the top and fascia.

BUILD THE BASE UNIT

Drill holes in the underside of the base unit top, insert dowel centers and lay the top on the base to mark it for drilling

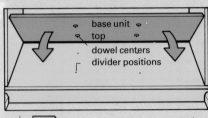

base unit
top
dowel centers
divider positions

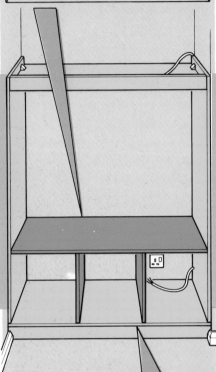

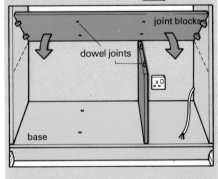

joint blocks

dowel joints

base

The top of the base unit must be the same width as the top and attached to the sides in the same way, but the dividers must be cut and fitted with dowel centers first. Drill and fit the dowels before attaching the base unit top.

FIT THE DISPLAY SHELVES

Use a level to set the shelf position, then mark the dowel positions

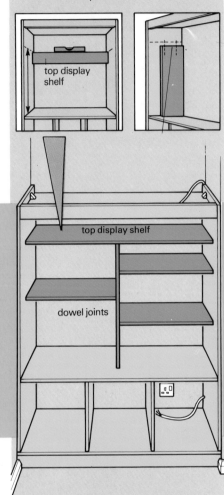

top display shelf

top display shelf

dowel joints

Make dowel joints on the end of shelves and supports. 'Spring' in the shelves

Cut the display shelves and their supports. Don't forget to allow for the thickness of intervening supports. Use dowel centers to mark dowel positions. Drill and fit dowels to project by ⅜in; 'spring' in the shelves.

FIT OUT THE BASE UNIT

If you fit a door, use a piano hinge. Cut the door from a full board

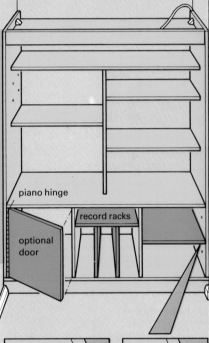

piano hinge

record racks

optional door

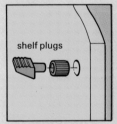

shelf plugs

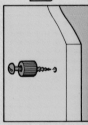

Make the record rack in the same way as the base unit top and dividers – using dowels and joint blocks. Other shelves can be fitted with loose shelf plugs. If you want to fit a door, cut it to fit the size of the opening and hang it with a piano hinge for a firm fixing.

ADD THE FINISHING TOUCHES

You can support glass shelves with plastic shelf pins

Attach channeling top and bottom to carry the glass doors

plastic door slides

magnetic touch catch

glass pivot hinges

Hinged glass doors are an alternative. Fit them with brand name hinges and a magnetic catch

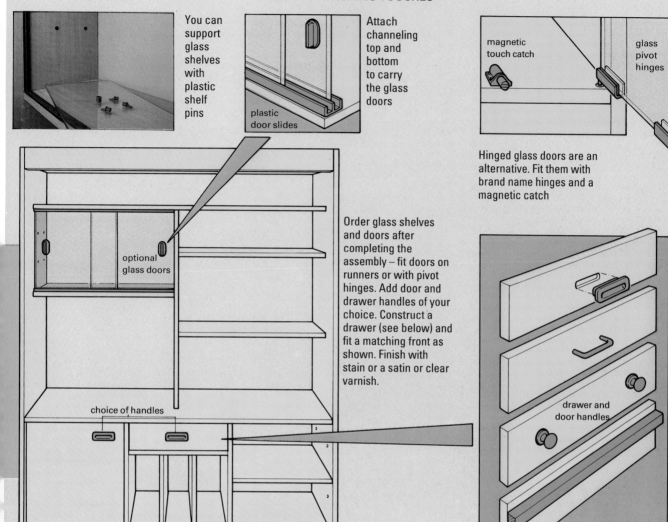

optional glass doors

Order glass shelves and doors after completing the assembly – fit doors on runners or with pivot hinges. Add door and drawer handles of your choice. Construct a drawer (see below) and fit a matching front as shown. Finish with stain or a satin or clear varnish.

choice of handles

drawer and door handles

★ Making Softwood or Plywood Drawers

Depending on the depth of the drawer, you can make the back, sides, and front from softwood or plywood. A false front to match the rest of the unit is attached by screwing into it through the front. The false front can sit flush with the front of the unit or overlap the drawer opening. The front and back are tacked and glued into rabbet joints cut in the sides. If the drawer is to run on its base, the bottom panel is tacked on top of cleats fixed to the sides, *a*, or set in a

groove cut into the sides, *b*; it is made to the full width of the opening and rests on hardwood runners or a panel beneath it. Alternatively it can rest on side runners, *c*; in this case the drawer is made narrower than the opening, with hardwood runners screwed to the drawer and unit, and the false front is made wider to conceal them; the bottom can be tacked and glued under the sides. To prevent the drawer from binding, insure that the corners are square and that it is a good fit. Ideally the front to back dimension should be greater than the width.

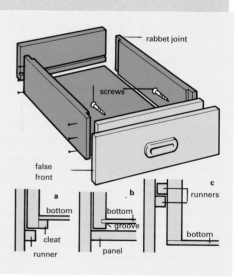

rabbet joint

screws

false front

a
bottom
cleat
runner

b
bottom
groove
panel

c
runners
bottom

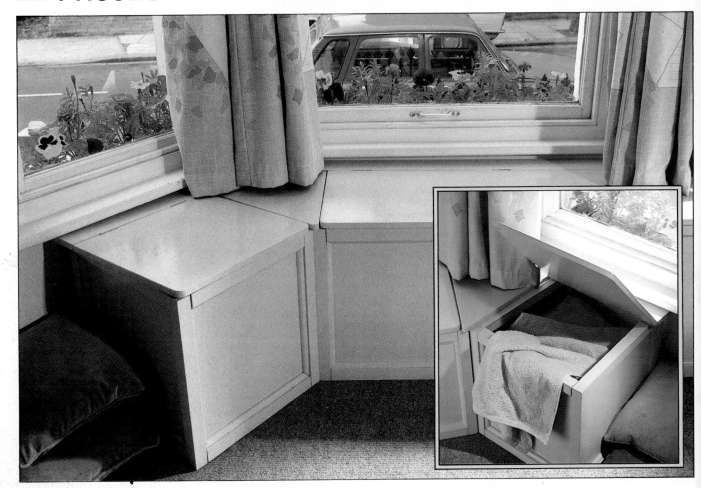

Window Seat Storage

When you're indoors on a bright sunny day, one of the nicest places to sit is at the window – especially if there's a comfy seat to rest on. This project shows you how to make just such a seat that also houses useful storage space.

A window seat is one of the few home improvement items that you can't buy 'off the shelf' at a lumber yard – they only look good if they are custom made to fit a specific window. The design for this seat is deceptively simple – the crucial part of the job is measuring and if you do

this accurately, you can be sure that you are well on the way to making a unique and good-looking unit that will benefit your home.

The plywood seats are hinged to sturdy sub-frames and when they are lifted up, masses of accessible storage space is revealed. The sub-frames are screwed to the walls and can be fixed to the floor as well for extra stability – there is no need to lift up any carpet as the frames can just stand on top.

You will need a few specialist tools if you are going to fit the seat into a bay. For instance, a T-bevel and a protractor will be invaluable for measuring and marking the internal angles. Apart from these, a general carpentry tool kit should see you safely through the job from start to finish.

CHECKLIST

Special tools
protractor and T-bevel
tenon saw and miter box
try square

Materials
¼in plywood
¾in plywood
1½in × 1½in softwood
4in × ⅝in softwood
½in quarter-round
⅜in dowels/butt hinges
1in brads
2in No. 8 flathead screws and plugs
joint blocks/wood glue

See Skills Guide
pp. 113, 123, 128, 132

BASIC WINDOW SEAT DESIGNS

The most obvious – and certainly the most traditional – place for a window seat is in a recessed bay, but there are other possible locations that are worth thinking about as well. For example, an adapted unit (below) could provide sturdy seating/storage in a child's playroom or in a cramped kitchen.

If you plan to fit the window seat into a bay, don't be scared by its awkward shape. Although the angles are seldom at a convenient 45 degrees, there is a simple way of measuring and marking, using a T-bevel and protractor – these two tools will enable you to cut the back trims and kite pieces (C) accurately.

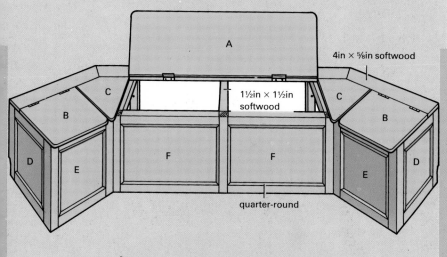

4in × ⅝in softwood

1½in × 1½in softwood

quarter-round

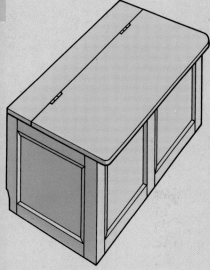

For a bay window seat, measure the width and depth of the recess before deciding on the height and depth of the units. You will find it easier to get an overall picture of the seat if you make a scale drawing on graph paper. As a general rule, keep the height of the seat between 12in and 18in; the depth is also variable but should not be greater than 18in. The plywood seat pieces (A and B) should overlap the leading edges of the sub-frames by about 1 in.

It is important that the wood is sanded smooth and sealed – on the outside at least. Several coats of polyurethane varnish or paint will give the best protection against accidental knocks.

MEASURING AND MARKING

Chalk an outline of the window seat on the floor or carpet

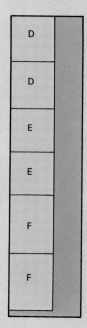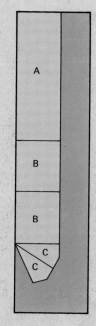

Mark the boards with care: allow for the thickness of the saw blade

The sub-frame cleats play an important visual as well as structural role, so mark and measure them accurately, using a try square to establish the face side and edge.

ASSEMBLE THE SUB-FRAMES

Dowels provide a strong and invisible fixing

⅜in dowel

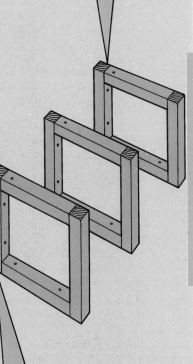

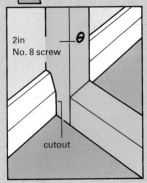

2in No. 8 screw

cutout

Cut notches out of the frames to allow for the baseboard

Assemble the sub-frames, using glued dowel joints (see Skills Guide p. 128). Use a profile gauge to transfer the outline of the baseboard on to the uprights and make the cutouts.

FIX THE CROSS-MEMBERS

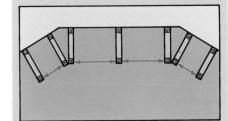

Tap the glued dowels home with a mallet before assembly

Stand the sub-frames in their positions in the bay window (top) – this will enable you to measure up the lengths of the cross-members accurately so that each one fits perfectly.

ANCHOR THE SUB-FRAMES

Check the frames are plumb before fixing

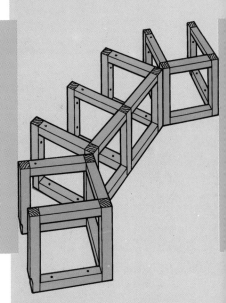

Use two screws per upright

Fix each back upright to the wall with at least two screws driven into wallplugs. For extra stability, you can also screw the frames to the floor but this may prove tricky if it is made from concrete.

16

PIN THE PANELS

Saw the molding in a miter box

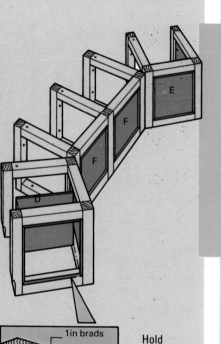

1in brads

D

cutout for baseboard

Hold each panel in place with eight brads

Brad the lengths of molding inside the sub-frames and punch the heads into the wood. Hold the plywood panels tight against the beading with a series of brads driven only half way in.

FIT THE BACK TRIM

You will need a T-bevel and protractor for the internal angles

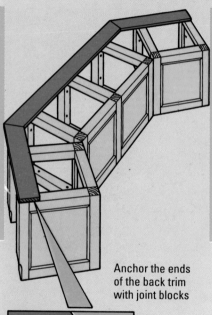

Anchor the ends of the back trim with joint blocks

joint block

Measure the angle between walls with a T-bevel, then divide the angle in half and mark a cutting line with a protractor

HINGE THE TOPS

Rabbet the hinges into the tops

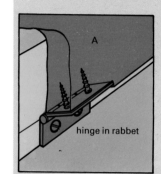

hinge in rabbet

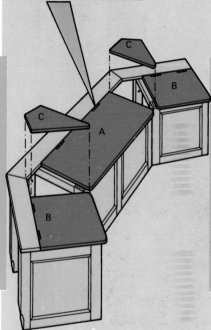

Fix the kite pieces (C) to the sub-frames by screwing up from underneath. Finish the units with several coats of paint or polyurethane varnish

★ **Marking profiles**

To use a profile gauge, press the row of steel spines against the object (in this case a baseboard): the spines will slide out, imitating the outline of the object in detail.
To transfer the outline, hold the gauge against the workpiece.

CHECKLIST

Tools
tape measure
try square
electric drill and bits (including ¼in
    dowelling bit)
circular saw
level
bradawl
screwdrivers
profile gauge (optional)
coping saw (optional)

Materials
½in veneered plywood
hardboard
¼in dowels
joint blocks
European hinges
1in wallboard screws
iron-on or self-stick veneer strips
cupboard knobs/hanging rail
paint or varnish

See Skills Guide pp. 113–5,
118, 123, 128, 134.

Custom-Built Wardrobe Units

Here's an easy-to-follow blueprint for wardrobe units that are just the answer if you have a bedroom that is short on clothes space. You can make just one freestanding unit or join a whole series together to form a comprehensive wall-to-wall system.

The advantage of a made-to-measure wardrobe that stretches from the floor to the ceiling is that it can have several layers of storage space: the top can be shelved off to create a cupboard for things like blankets and suitcases; the bottom can be filled up with drawers; and the space in between can be devoted entirely to hanging up clothes or can be fitted with shelves. This means that run-of-the-mill cupboards and chests of drawers can be replaced by one integral unit.

The wardrobe design described here consists of units so that you can make anything from one tall, narrow hanging cupboard to a whole set of inter-connecting ones that fill a whole wall. An advantage of built-in wardrobes is that they are unobtrusive in a bedroom.

The drawers can be constructed from plywood or softwood, with plywood bases. They are supported on hardwood side runners.

Dowels and joint blocks are used to support the shelves which you can space out according to your needs.

If you want to build the units into an alcove, or want a complete row of fitted wardrobes, you can adapt the scribing and cutting techniques that are described on pages 9–13.

DESIGN OPTIONS FOR WARDROBE UNITS

MEASURING

The wide units should be twice the width of the narrow ones.

Divide tall units into horizontal bays and fit independent doors. Drawers can be hidden behind the doors if recessed handles are fitted

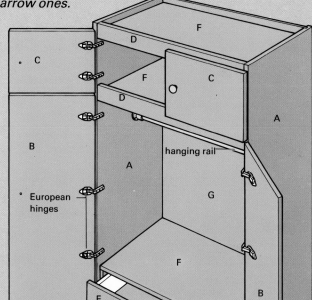

hanging rail

European hinges

recessed handles

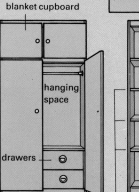

blanket cupboard

hanging space

drawers

double unit

optional shelves

single unit

Ideally, the units should stretch from floor to ceiling but if you are not making fitted units, allow 2in headroom

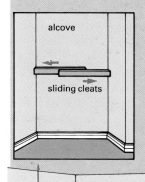

alcove

sliding cleats

If fitting into an alcove, gauge the width with two sliding 1in × 2in cleats

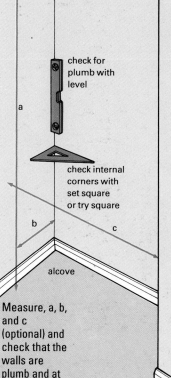

check for plumb with level

a

check internal corners with set square or try square

b   c

alcove

Measure, a, b, and c (optional) and check that the walls are plumb and at right angles to each other

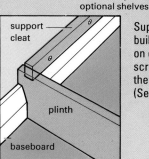

support cleat

plinth

baseboard

Support built-in units on cleats screwed to the walls. (See pp 9–13)

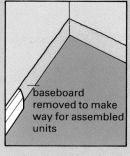

baseboard removed to make way for assembled units

Freestanding units can fit neatly into a corner if you cut back the baseboard

Cut a ³⁄₁₆in deep groove on the inside faces of the side panels for the back piece (G)

Decide on what sort of units you want – narrow units are best divided up with shelves, wider ones can be fitted with drawers, shelves and hanging rails.

The widest a double unit can be is 4ft – the width of a sheet. For a freestanding unit, 3ft is ideal but aim to balance the width with the height.

Cut the grooves with a circular saw – they should be ³⁄₈in in from the back edges.

2

ASSEMBLE THE DRAWER

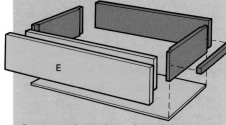

Construct plywood or softwood drawers with side runners (see page 13). The false fronts (E) cover the panels (H)

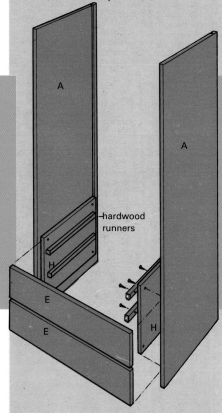

hardwood runners

The drawers have to be attached to separate panels (H) so that they can slide right into the unit, allowing the doors to close.

Fix the ⅝in square hardwood runners to the drawer panels (H) using 1½in chipboard screws

side runner

counterbored holes

3

ADD THE SHELVES

Mark the positions of the shelves on the side panels – they must be square to the edges

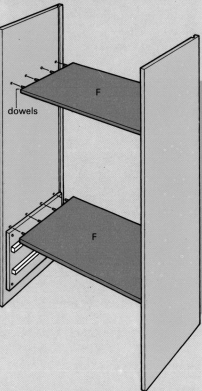

dowels

The support shelves use dowels, the others have joint blocks

Wrap tape ¼in from the end of the bit and use it as a depth gauge. Keep the drill vertical

Fit each shelf using eight dowels. Align the dowel holes using dowelling pins (see page 128), then fit glued dowels to secure.

4

FIX THE PLINTHS

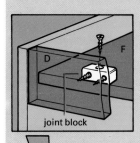

Fix the top and bottom shelves and the plinth bars with joint blocks

joint block

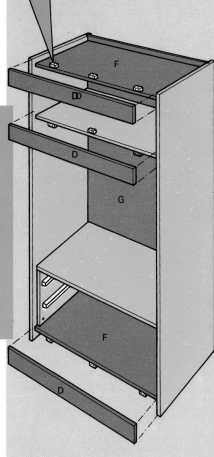

Add the shelves to the panels while the unit's on its side.

Slide in the back piece after fitting the shelves

You will need at least one other person to help you slide the back piece along its grooves – one pulling, the other pushing.

FIT THE UNITS

Use T-nut connectors to join units together

two-piece panel connecting bolts

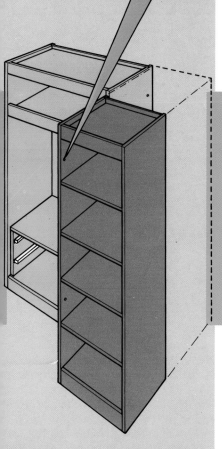

After fitting one unit into a corner, slide in the others

Slip the units into place on plastic sheeting

Tall units are awkward to move because there is little headroom. A clever way around this problem is to slide in the units on plastic.

FIX THE HANDLES

Stick recessed handles to the drawers with PVA glue

If you are fitting recessed handles, drill out the wells with a flat bit

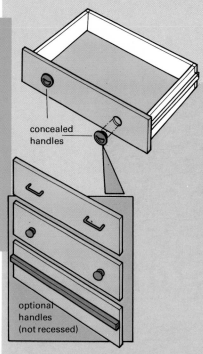

concealed handles

optional handles (not recessed)

There are many handle options and they are all fixed differently.

HANG THE DOORS

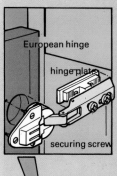

European hinge

hinge plate

securing screw

Attach the two parts of each hinge separately, then bring them together

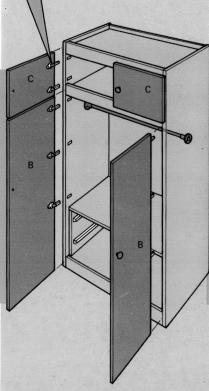

Screw the hanging rail inside the unit before fitting concealed hinges and handles.

CHECKLIST

Materials
¾in chipboard shelves
1 × 1 softwood cleats
½in chipboard (doors)
casement molding
2in finishing nails
1¼in No. 8 flathead screws
1½in No. 8 flathead screws
wallplugs
PVA woodworking adhesive
door stays
1½in brass hinges
knobs or handles
wood filler
magnetic catches (optional)

Tools
electric drill and bits
crosscut saw or saber saw
level
screwdrivers
countersink bit
backsaw and miter box
tape measure
putty knife

See Skills Guide pp. 113–4, 118, 123–5, 130, 132, 139.

Overhead Storage Units

No matter how cramped your home, if you really look, you will probably find it actually contains a lot of wasted space – the area above a doorway, for example. Here's a simple unit that turns that particular gap into useful storage space.

It seems ironic that the more things are invented to go in the home, the less room the designers of new houses appear to allow to accommodate them. As for older houses, they tend to become more and more cluttered every day. The net result is that in homes old and new storage space is now at a real premium, and few people can afford to let any opportunity to increase it pass

them by.

But simply adding storage space at random isn't enough. The kind of storage you provide has to suit the kind of things you want to store. In particular you must aim to make the odds and ends you use most frequently readily accessible. That may sound a tall order, but oddly enough, it is rarely this kind of everyday item that causes the biggest

storage problem. The hardest things to find a home for, are often the sort of things you use perhaps once a month or even less – things that don't really warrant a slice of your precious 'everyday' storage quota, yet which would make life far too difficult if they were to be tucked away in a corner of the attic.

Finding space isn't really all that difficult – take a look at all that wasted space above one of your home's doorways for example. All that's required to turn it into just the sort of medium term storage space you need is an easy-to-build unit like the one shown here. True, it won't take very large or very heavy items, and you will need a stool or small step ladder to reach into the cupboards, but you'll find it none the less useful for that – it's ideal for things like blankets.

STORAGE UNIT DESIGNS

This convenient overhead storage unit has been specially designed for use in the sort of small rooms where storage space is most precious – small bedrooms, tiny bathrooms, and so on.

The unit uses two cupboard sizes – those with side hung doors on the lower tier cope with most small items, while the large top hung doors on the upper tier are for rarely used bulky items.

CUTTING OUT

To allow for the fact that the alcove may be out of square, measure the shelf widths in several places using a pair of 'sliding' wooden cleats as a gauge.

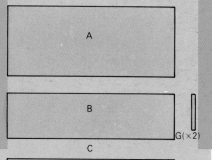

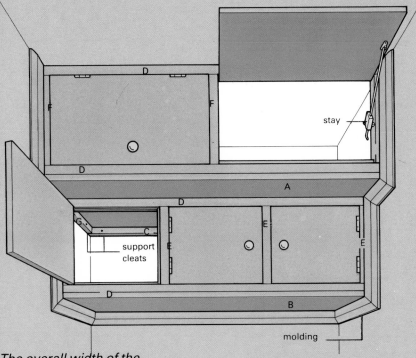

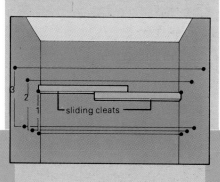

The overall width of the illustrated unit is about 60in but you can tailor the dimensions to fit into your smallest room. However to minimize the risk of the shelves bowing, treat this dimension as a maximum. If you want a wider unit, additional support must be provided, in the form of conventional shelf brackets, though these will make it far more difficult to give the unit a really neat built-in finish. The unit's depth is rather more flexible, but do remember that it can be extremely difficult to reach right to the back of a very deep cupboard when it is high up on the wall. Deep cupboards can also look unsightly in some rooms, so, for this reason, keep the lower section of the unit shallower (about 16in) than the deep cupboard above (about 24in).

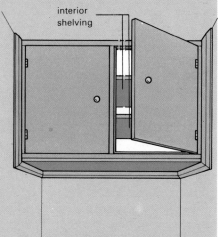

Of course, there is no need for you to stick rigidly to the design. If you prefer – or if it better suits your storage needs – you can construct the unit as a slightly taller, single tier cupboard fitted with twin doors and shelves.

To stop the saber saw chipping the surface veneer, stick masking tape along line

Work out the exact sizes of the various components illustrated above from the dimensions of the alcove above the door, then cut out as accurately as possible with a saber saw a lot quicker and easier.

TOP SHELF SUPPORTS

Cut the side support cleats so their length plus the width of the lower cupboard frames equals the depth of the bottom shelf

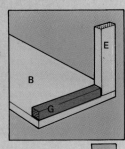

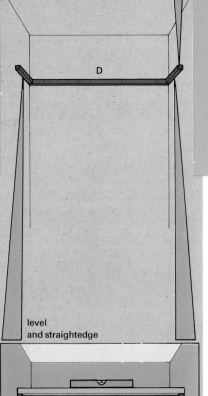

level and straightedge

Attach the wooden cleats that support the unit's top shelf to the wall using screw and wallplugs. Use a level (and at the front a long straightedge) to check that they are absolutely horizontal.

LOWER SHELF SUPPORTS

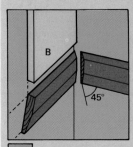

Be sure to miter the side moldings correctly – their short upper edges should match the depth of the lower shelf

molding

Cut the miters using a backsaw and miter box, making sure you have the miters the right way round

As with the upper support cleats, insure the moldings supporting the bottom shelf are level. Check, too, that the two sets of shelf supports are correctly spaced, remembering to allow for the thickness of the lower shelf. Cut the molding miters neatly using a backsaw and miter box.

ATTACHING THE SHELVES

To make it easier to screw the shelves in place, pre-drill with countersunk pilot holes

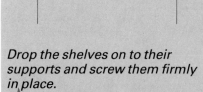

Drop the shelves on to their supports and screw them firmly in place.

★ Tight corners

Driving woodscrews into awkward corners isn't easy – unless you use an off-set screwdriver.

5
ADD DOOR FRAMES

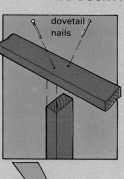

The unit's door frames are simply butt jointed, glued and dovetail nailed together. Make sure they are square and a snug fit within the alcove

dovetail nails

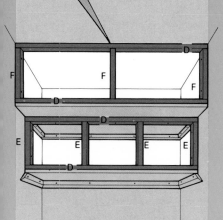

F   F   F   D   D   E   E   E   E   D

Screw the assembled frames to the shelves, making sure their respective front edges are perfectly aligned

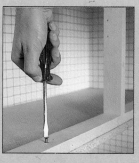

Assemble the softwood frames that form the front of the unit. These are simply glued and nailed together, then attached to the walls and ceiling with screws and wallplugs before being screwed to the shelves. It is important that the door openings are absolutely square, and the frames fit snugly.

6
HANGING THE DOORS

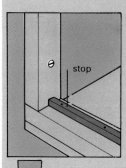

stop

To provide the upper half of the unit's doors with a stop, simply glue and tack the wood to the main softwood frame

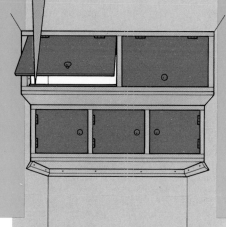

Before attaching the doors permanently in place, attach with one screw per hinge, and check that they open smoothly

The unit is now ready to receive its doors. To make access to the storage space easier, those for the upper set of cupboards are top hung. Take special care that all the doors open and close smoothly, and that they are set sufficiently square not to open by themselves; adjust as necessary.

7
FINISHING OFF

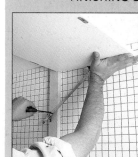

Screw door stays in place to hold the doors of the top cupboards open while you reach inside

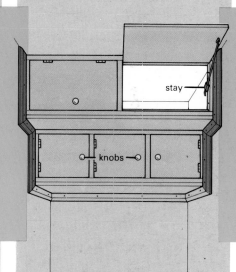

stay

knobs

Use woodfiller to neaten up any gaps between molding and unit before painting

To complete the unit, all that remains is to add additional moldings to disguise the joins between unit and walls. These can be either screwed and plugged or nailed in place. Use woodfiller to neaten up any remaining gaps, and cover the nail or screw heads, before painting.

Understair Desk

The space under the stairs is often one of the most wasted areas inside a house. This project comes to terms with the awkward shape and converts it into a practical and good looking work area.

The triangle of space underneath a staircase is very difficult to utilize fully because it is such an awkward shape. More often than not, it is partitioned off for use as a cupboard but this solution is seldom totally satisfactory because, whereas one end of the cupboard is tall and spacious, the further reaches tend to be dark and almost totally inaccessible.

This project approaches this tricky area in a new way: instead of closing it off, it opens it out into a practical work/storage space. The design consists of a triangular desk – two corners rest on supporting shelf units and one edge is braced by a cleat screwed to the wall. A third shelf unit insures that you will have ample space for the materials you need there.

The design is fully adaptable and you can tailor-make the units to fit under your stairs no matter how steeply they slope. And, if you incorporate a storage cart (see pages 64–67) in the design, the entire area under the stairs can be put to good use.

The shelf units are easy to construct from ¾in plywood, using either dowels or joint blocks as shelf supports. The desk top is made from two sheets of ½in particleboard – two sheets are used to insure that no ugly attachments are visible on the top: the bottom sheet is screwed to its supports, then the second sheet is glued on top. All the exposed edges are trimmed with hardwood strips for neatness.

There is no reason why you can't paint the whole construction but an original finish for the desk top is colored felt (as illustrated) which you can either glue or staple in place. You shouldn't have any trouble buying felt – most department stores sell rolls of it in a wide range of colors.

The triangular shape of the desk top is one way of making sure that there is plenty of leg room underneath and that the work area is as large as you need. However, you can make a square-shaped desk (below) if it is more suitable – in fact, you can build this simpler unit against virtually any wall for use as a desk, dressing table or workbench.

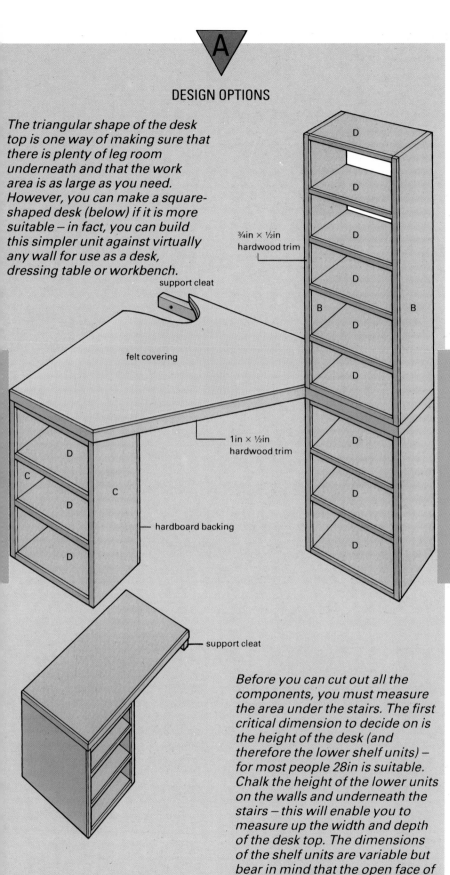

support cleat

¾in × ½in hardwood trim

felt covering

B B

1in × ½in hardwood trim

D

C

C

D

D

hardboard backing

support cleat

Before you can cut out all the components, you must measure the area under the stairs. The first critical dimension to decide on is the height of the desk (and therefore the lower shelf units) – for most people 28in is suitable. Chalk the height of the lower units on the walls and underneath the stairs – this will enable you to measure up the width and depth of the desk top. The dimensions of the shelf units are variable but bear in mind that the open face of the desk should be about 3ft wide. The top unit reaches from the desk to the ceiling.

Mark out the width and depth of the desk at this stage but leave the final shaping of the top until after you have cut out the shelf components – see stage 2.

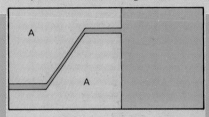

Once you have decided on the optimum size of the shelves, saw one out and use it as a template for the others. Not only is this the easiest way of marking out but it insures that the shelves are identical to one another.

CUT OUT COMPONENTS

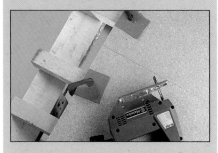

Before you cut out the particleboard desk tops, support the sheet on either side of the cutting line with stout wood supports to prevent it trapping the blade.

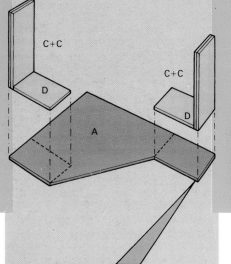

hardwood trim

A

cutting line

Unless the protruding edge butts against a wall make allowances for the trim

Use a shelf and two side panels to complete the marking out of the desk tops. Cut out the pieces with a power saber saw.

Unless the protruding edge of the desk is to butt against a wall, allow for the trim.

ASSEMBLE SHELF UNITS

Tack and glue hardboard to the back of the front shelf unit

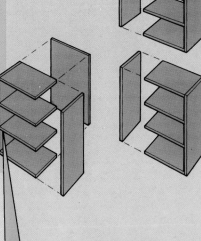

Attach the shelves with joint blocks or dowels

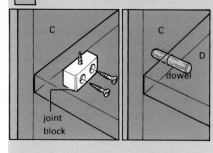

C

joint block

C

D

dowel

You can vary the spacings between shelves according to what you want to store. Attach the shelves using either joint blocks or dowels.

SECURE THE DESK TOP

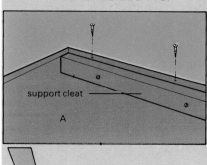

support cleat

A

The support cleat must be horizontal and at the same height as the shelf units

A

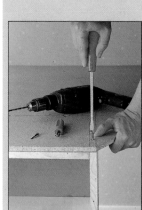

Drill countersunk clearance holes in the desk top before screwing it down

Screw the support cleat to the wall, then position the shelf units. Attach the top with screws driven through countersunk clearance holes.

COMPLETE THE DESK TOP

Spread a thin layer of contact adhesive on both surfaces using a notched spreader. Attach sides together when tacky

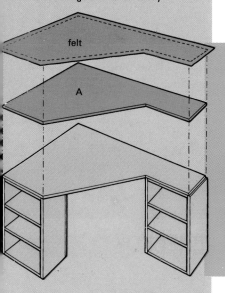

felt

A

Clamp the two pieces together for a good bond

Stick down the second sheet with impact adhesive and hold it in place with 1 × 2s and C clamps. Use glue or staples for the felt (see panel, right)

ADD THE TOP UNIT

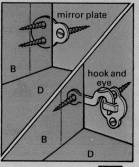

mirror plate

B

D

hook and eye

B

D

D

There are two ways of attaching the top shelf unit to the wall

It is not necessary to attach the top unit to the desk provided it is anchored to the wall

TRIM THE EDGES

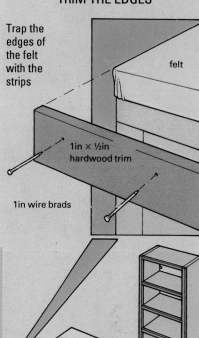

Trap the edges of the felt with the strips

felt

1in × ½in hardwood trim

1in wire brads

¾in × ½in trim

Cover all the exposed edges with strips of hardwood. Tack and glue the strips in place

★ *Quick fixing methods*

A staple gun *is an invaluable tool for joining fabrics and even thin laminates to wooden framework and man-made boards*

*Electrically operated **glue guns** are a comparatively new invention. The glue bonds well – and very quickly – to most materials*

Kitchen Island Unit

Planning a large kitchen isn't easy. If you're not careful, you can leave acres of empty space in the middle of the room and face a long walk between counters. One way around the problem is to put in an island.

People with small kitchens don't always realize just how lucky they are. Fitting the units and appliances you want into a more spacious room may be easier in principle, but is rarely so in practice. Making sure that everything you need for cooking, washing dishes and so on is within reach can be a real problem. All too often, no matter how carefully you arrange the units around the kitchen walls, you find yourself having to walk from one 'work station' to another, and although the distances involved may not be great, in the course of a day they soon add up.

But there are ways you can get around the problem. One of the simplest is to make use of the center of the room with an island or peninsular unit. In addition to providing the kitchen with a much needed visual focal point, it can give you the counter space and storage you need just when you need it, to say nothing of its potential as a very handy breakfast bar. Adding an island unit need not be a terribly expensive solution, either. Using modern materials and jointing techniques, it's easy enough to build one yourself.

CHECKLIST

Tools
Ruler and pencil
Try square and marking knife
Crosscut saw or saber saw
Screwdrivers and bradawl
Plane or surform tool
C-clamps/Laminate cutter

Materials
Plastic laminate
⅝in melamine chipboard
⅝in plain chipboard
1 × 2 softwood
Knock-down hardware
Recessed door hinges
Magnetic spring catches
¾in and ½in No. 8 screws
Self-stick edging strip
Wood and contact adhesive

See Skills Guide
pp. 114–5, 134.

KITCHEN ISLAND DESIGNS

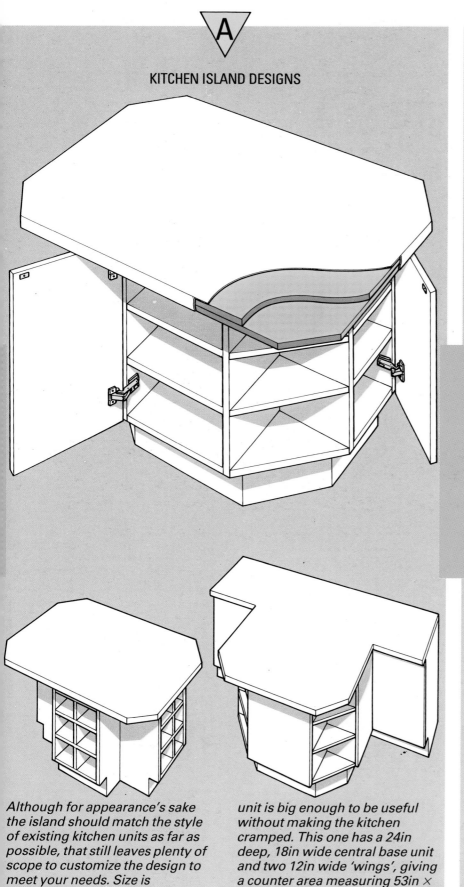

CUTTING THE PARTS

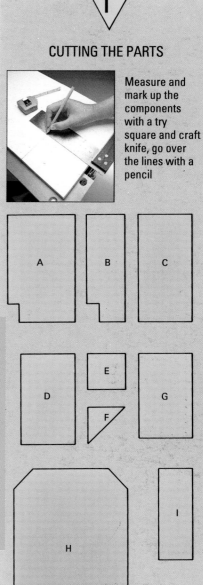

Measure and mark up the components with a try square and craft knife, go over the lines with a pencil

Although for appearance's sake the island should match the style of existing kitchen units as far as possible, that still leaves plenty of scope to customize the design to meet your needs. Size is important, though – insure the

unit is big enough to be useful without making the kitchen cramped. This one has a 24in deep, 18in wide central base unit and two 12in wide 'wings', giving a counter area measuring 53in × 37in.

Having decided on the unit's exact design and size, cut the components for ⅝in thick chipboard. Use plain chipboard for the doors and worktop; melamine or laminate-covered board for the rest. Mark this up as carefully as possible, insuring the various components are absolutely square before cutting them out. For a clean edge mark all cut lines with a sharp knife, scoring right through any veneer, then neaten off the finished cut edges with sandpaper.

THE CENTRAL UNIT

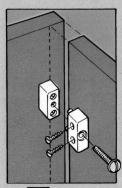

Carefully position the joint blocks and screw to unit back and sides ready for assembly

2-piece joint blocks

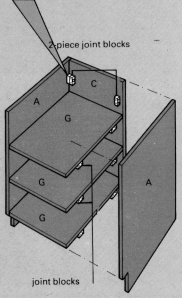

joint blocks

With the central carcase assembled, drop in the shelves and screw to their support blocks

Assemble the central unit, using joint blocks to join the sides and back (three per side) and to support the shelves. Attaching all blocks to the sides first makes the job very much easier.

EXTENDING THE WINGS

Use the shelves as a gauge when marking shelf positions and upright spacings

2-piece joint blocks

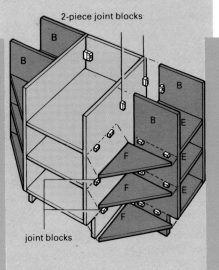

joint blocks

Draw in the shelf positions and attach the shelf support blocks before assembling the unit wings

Attach the 'wing' uprights to the center unit with blocks, and again support the shelves on blocks. For accuracy, use the rear cupboard shelves to space the uprights correctly.

ATTACHING THE PLINTH

Saw the kickboard support blocks to shape, then finish with a plane or surform tool

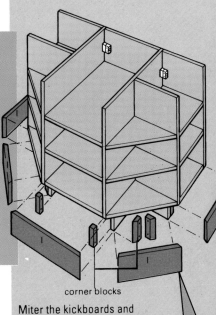

corner blocks

Miter the kickboards and reinforcing blocks at an angle of 22½ degrees

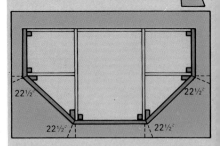

22½   22½

22½   22½

Glue all kickboards in place, reinforcing the joints between them and the unit uprights with softwood blocks glued and screwed in place. Cut the block and kickboard angles accurately.

ATTACHING THE COUNTER

Spread adhesive evenly over the two pieces forming the table top using a notched spreader

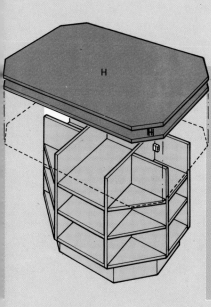

Clamp the table top together until the adhesive has set protecting the surface with scrap wood

The table top, which is attached to the unit using 1-piece shelf support blocks, consists of two sheets of chipboard glued together. You may need to plane the edges of the resulting sandwich flush.

ADDING THE LAMINATE

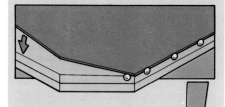

Use thumb tacks as an aid to positioning the laminate

plastic laminate

The edge of the top can be laminated or finished with molding or iron-on edging strip

The counter can now be finished with plastic laminate glued in place using a contact adhesive. The counter edges may also be laminated, though it is easier to use iron-on edging strip.

ATTACHING THE DOORS

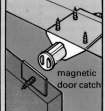

magnetic door catch

The doors are hung on European sprung hinges and fitted with magnetic catches

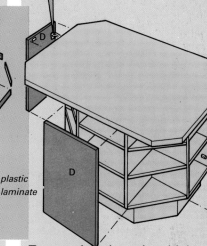

plastic laminate

To complete the unit, add the doors to the central and wing cupboards

★ *Cutting laminates*

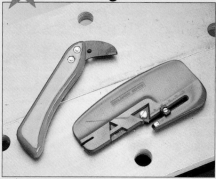

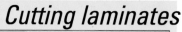

Buy a laminate cutter (left) and an edge trimming tool too.

Breakfast Bar

Tall, narrow spaces are among the hardest to fill in kitchens and small apartments. This project gives you useful storage space combined with an eating area which folds out of the way.

In very small kitchens or apartments where space is at a premium, it is important to use what room is available as efficiently as possible. This design makes use of those awkward vertical places which are difficult to use properly unless you fill them with stoves and refrigerators.

Because the eating and working surface folds down (but stows neatly out of the way when not in use), the breakfast bar provides a practical table when you need it but doesn't get in the way when you don't. In fact, this design is so space-efficient that you might even feel that it's worth building it to replace another, less useful piece of furniture.

Another useful feature is that almost all of the components can be cut from sheets of the same width which makes life simpler.

CHECKLIST

Tools
saber saw
drill and bits
backsaw and miter box
chisel
steel tape measure
screwdrivers
C-clamps
try square
hole saw and an iron

Materials
sheets of ⅝in coated chipboard
Softwood: ½in × ½in, 1 × 1
and 1 × 4
joint blocks
flushdoor hinges
plastic roller catches
iron-on edging for chipboard
paint or varnish

See Skills Guide pp.
114–5, 118, 125, 130, 133.

THE BREAKFAST BAR'S DESIGN

Construction of the breakfast bar is simple as all the components apart from the plinth, fold-down bar frame and catch rail are in sheet material. Plastic-coated chipboard such as melamine is the most attractive and practical material for use in the kitchen as it wipes clean but you could equally well use plywood as long as you finish it with paint or varnish so that liquids will not soak in if you spill anything. The only other materials you need are softwood, the roller catches and special double-cranked cabinet hinges.

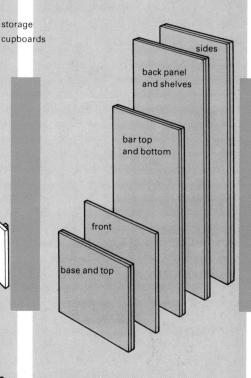

shelves

storage cupboards

drop-down bar

plinth

There are no difficult joints to make apart from the miters on the plinth unit, as all the sheet components are held together with plastic joint blocks.

As long as you keep the height of the bar roughly the same as shown here (35in), it is an easy matter to modify the size and shape of the bar and the number and placing of the shelves to suit your particular need or application. It's easiest to keep the shelves and bar to a standard 2ft wide sheet of board as this won't entail so much cutting.

hinging bar

The doors provide access to storage space where you can have as many shelves as you like. The small illustration on the right shows the side panel cut back to form an extra shelf.

CUT THE COMPONENTS

Most of the panels and shelves can be cut from sheets of a similar size to each other without much waste. The top and bottom panels sit between the sides of the unit, so they are the same width as the shelves which minimizes cutting. All the internal panels can come out of sheets of the same width.

sides

back panel and shelves

bar top and bottom

front

base and top

Cut the sheets with a saber saw, using a clamped-down cleat as a cutting guide. Tape the coating to prevent it chipping.

② ASSEMBLE THE BASE

After cutting the sheets to size, cover the exposed chipboard edges which will show with iron-on strip. The simplest way to build the breakfast bar is to make the base unit first and then attach the side panel to it – by doing this you'll find it easier to get the shelves in later.

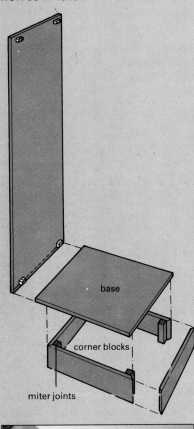

base

corner blocks

miter joints

Cut miters on the plinth members – for extra strength the corners are reinforced with blocks the same depth as the plinth.

③ MAKE THE BAR

Screw the hinges into place. You may need to recess the hinge plates

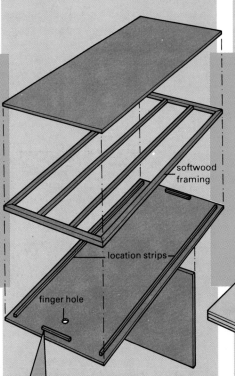

softwood framing

location strips

finger hole

The small strips serve to locate the frame

Assemble the bar itself before you attach it to the front panel with hinges. Clamp the bar and frame 'sandwich' while the adhesive dries. Cut a finger hole in the bar bottom as a purchase point.

④ ADD INTERMEDIATE PANELS

Screw the joint blocks in to place to hold the shelves and dividers

joint block above shelf

The middle shelf also has joint blocks above

Fit the middle shelf, top panel and vertical divider which hold the bar steady when open. Then fit the bar and front panel. Next, slot in and fix the lower shelf with its two dividers.

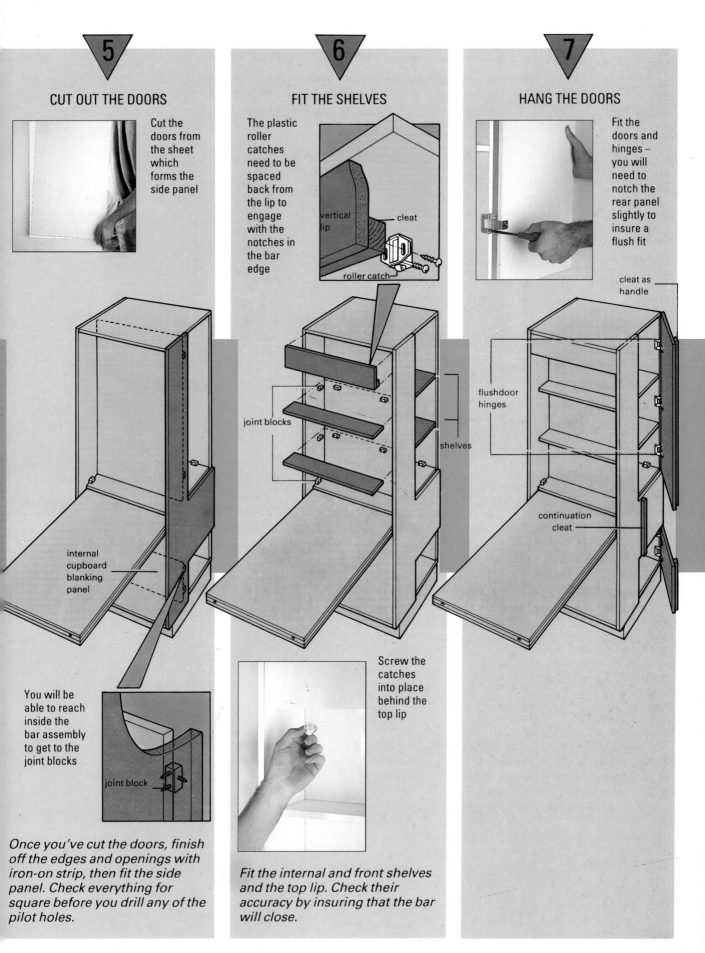

5 CUT OUT THE DOORS

Cut the doors from the sheet which forms the side panel

internal cupboard blanking panel

You will be able to reach inside the bar assembly to get to the joint blocks

joint block

Once you've cut the doors, finish off the edges and openings with iron-on strip, then fit the side panel. Check everything for square before you drill any of the pilot holes.

6 FIT THE SHELVES

The plastic roller catches need to be spaced back from the lip to engage with the notches in the bar edge

vertical lip

cleat

roller catch

joint blocks

shelves

Screw the catches into place behind the top lip

Fit the internal and front shelves and the top lip. Check their accuracy by insuring that the bar will close.

7 HANG THE DOORS

Fit the doors and hinges – you will need to notch the rear panel slightly to insure a flush fit

cleat as handle

flushdoor hinges

continuation cleat

Split-Level Floor

Open spaces which you don't need can be rather boring, even if they do give the room the impression of being larger than it really is. Splitting the room into well-defined areas on different levels makes all of the space more useful.

If you don't want to go to the trouble of constructing new walls or screens in order to split off certain areas of the room, you can always attack the problem from a different angle. By altering the level of part of the room – and by using the shelves as a boundary – you can alter the room by isolating part of it at a fraction of the cost of any alternative methods.

You could make the platform to do this almost any size you like – from one which only houses shelves to one large enough to double as a full-sized dining area. The shelves themselves can go anywhere as they are a separate structure which is held to the outside of the box by screws.

Although the idea of making a platform with steps incorporated into it might sound daunting, the basic structure is only a large box. The steps – like the shelves – are a separate structure which is screwed to the base unit.

As the platform is entirely free-standing there's no need to anchor it to the wall, so if you have enough helpers it can be easily moved, even when complete. There are no complicated joints to make – the main structure is simply screwed together while the shelves are dowel-jointed and glued, so construction should pose no particular carpentry problems.

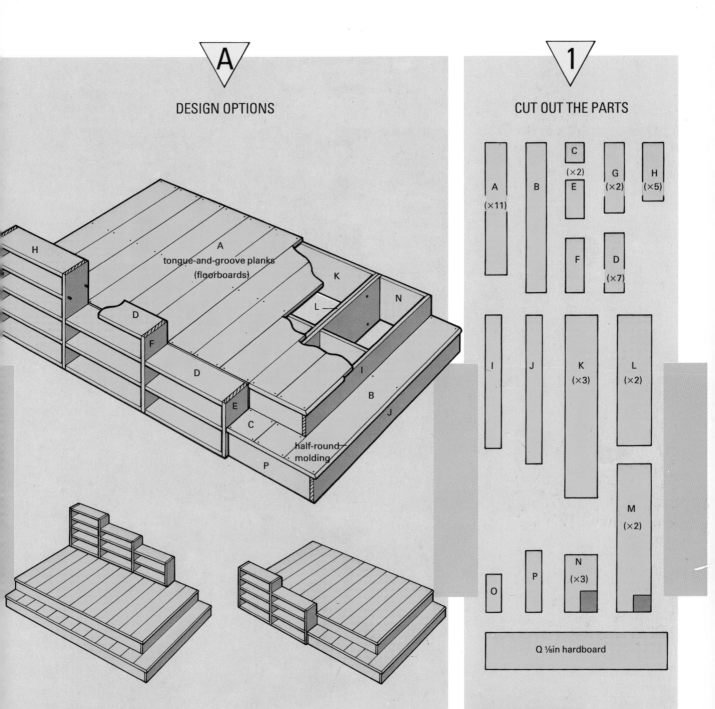

The platform is based around a simple box made from ½in plywood, with the steps and shelves attached to it by screws. You can make the platform more or less any size or height you like, although as sizes increase it would be prudent to include a few more internal stiffening ribs. If you increase the height of the platform you'll have to add more steps to reach the top of it, each step ideally being less than 8in high. Remember too that the height of the risers should be less than the depth of the treads.

Where you put the shelves is up to you – at the front of the platform the shelves serve as a useful boundary, but if you want steps all the way around the outside of the platform the shelves will have to go at the back against one of the walls. You can leave the top shelves open or have them closed, but whatever happens you need the plywood panel at the back of the lower shelves, as this serves to attach the shelves to the main platform.

Clamp down parts M and N and cut out the step sections from them

Start off by marking out and cutting all the parts you'll need – a cleat clamped to the work will help you to keep the cuts straight, but you won't need this for the small step cut-outs.

ASSEMBLE THE MAIN BASE

Mark out and drill the dowel holes. Use dowel centers to transfer marks across to corresponding parts

Once you've drilled the clearance holes, countersink them to house the screw heads

MAKE THE STEPS

Drill holes and test-fit, then apply glue and assemble joints

For parts which will have to take the most stress, such as the step assemblies, use glue as well as the screws to hold the joints together. Test for fit before you apply the glue.

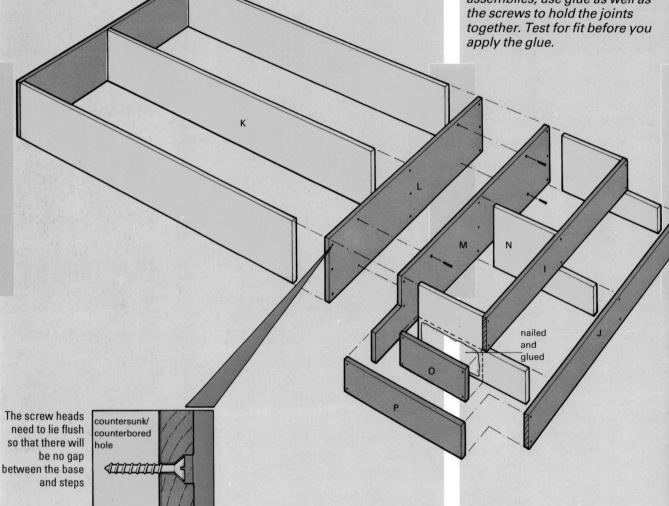

The screw heads need to lie flush so that there will be no gap between the base and steps

countersunk/counterbored hole

nailed and glued

Once you've cut the base parts out, check them against each other to make sure that they are the same height. Mark out and drill clearance holes through parts L first, then transfer the positions

to the longer parts K. You'll find it easier if you drill pilot holes for the screws as well. The screw heads need to be flush, so countersink and (if necessary) counterbore them.

With the base unit and steps made up, attach them together with screws (see picture opposite). For ease of handling, don't glue the sections together. Glue and nail on part O before you add P.

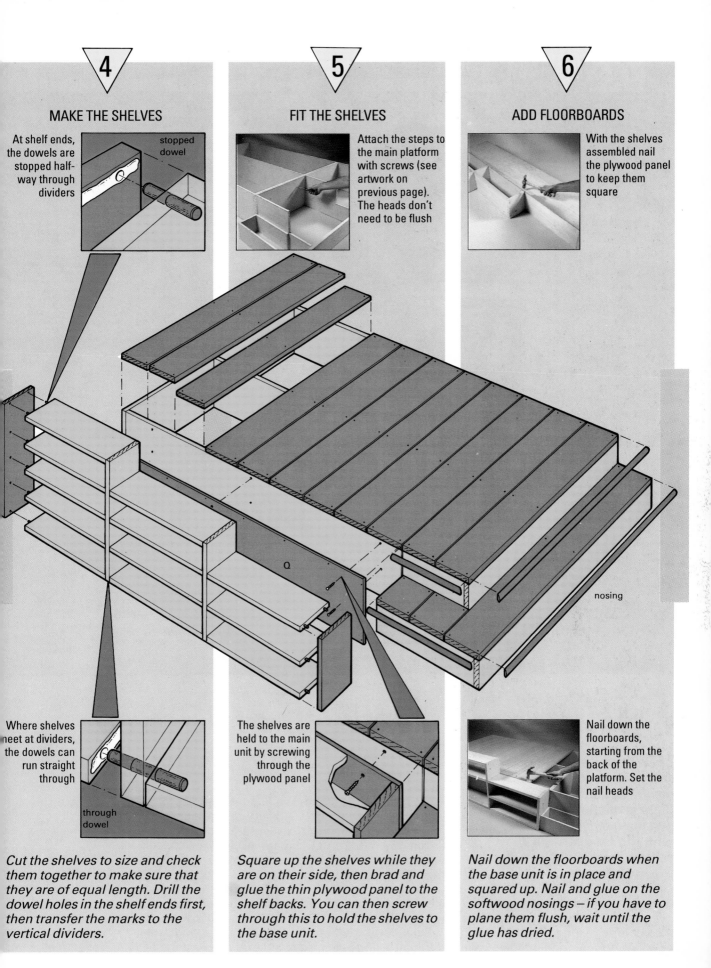

MAKE THE SHELVES

At shelf ends, the dowels are stopped half-way through dividers

stopped dowel

Where shelves meet at dividers, the dowels can run straight through

through dowel

Cut the shelves to size and check them together to make sure that they are of equal length. Drill the dowel holes in the shelf ends first, then transfer the marks to the vertical dividers.

FIT THE SHELVES

Attach the steps to the main platform with screws (see artwork on previous page). The heads don't need to be flush

The shelves are held to the main unit by screwing through the plywood panel

Square up the shelves while they are on their side, then brad and glue the thin plywood panel to the shelf backs. You can then screw through this to hold the shelves to the base unit.

ADD FLOORBOARDS

With the shelves assembled nail the plywood panel to keep them square

nosing

Nail down the floorboards, starting from the back of the platform. Set the nail heads

Nail down the floorboards when the base unit is in place and squared up. Nail and glue on the softwood nosings – if you have to plane them flush, wait until the glue has dried.

Putting Up New Banisters

Apart from its functional role, a staircase can also be a decorative feature. But if your flight is dangerously rickety or just plain ugly, refurbishing it with the aid of ornate kit components could be a step in the right direction.

Renewing an unstable or unattractive staircase balustrade is not just a means of investing it with a brand new look, the components also form a vital safety barrier. Various types of kit are available from lumber yards.

Most domestic staircases feature supporting newel posts at the foot and head of the flight, which are linked by a handrail and braced with vertical balusters, solid panelling, rails or wrought ironwork, and it's these parts which can be replaced with new pieces in turned, shaped wood.

Balustrade kits are available in different woods which can either be painted or varnished to match your decor. The spindles, newel posts and hand rails are available in a choice of design and all the components are made in such a way that they can be adapted to any style and type of staircase.

Putting up balusters used to be a job of a professional carpenter, but the kits are simple to use, needing only modest carpentry skills. All the hardware and brackets that you need to attach the handrail to the newel posts are available at your supplier.

1 What the job involves

Once you've chosen the style of components, installation on a straight flight involves:

● cutting down the existing newel post to take a new newel center

● glueing the spigot of a turned newel center into a hole cut in the top of the newel base

● screwing the channelled base rail to the string

● cutting the hand rail to match the base rail and attaching it between newels using special metal brackets

● trimming the spindles to fit between base and hand rails

● arranging the spindles between the rails and retaining them with nail-on spacer fillets

BEFORE YOU START

● Familiarize yourself with staircase construction, so you know which parts you will be dealing with, and how they are attached to the main structure. In a basic straight staircase the steps – which include both the treads and the risers

– are located in housing joints cut in the inside faces of inclined sides called strings, and are held by wedges. The strings are either attached top and bottom to joists, or screwed against a wall or between two walls of a stairwell.

● Identify the staircase format you have, as this determines exactly what components you need. There are basically seven formats: straight flight; straight flight with winders; straight flight with side-fixed newels; quarter turn landing; half turn landing; open well half turn with 90° turn; and top landing with 180° turn.

● Choose the balustrade components. For a simple straight flight all you'll need are: lengths of hand and base rail; landing and bottom newel bases and centers including decorative caps which come in a variety of sizes and shapes; bottom and top brackets plus plugs; and spindles and fillets. For more complex staircase formats

you may need intermediate newels, which accommodate two risers, plus top and bottom brackets. Where there's a straight landing at the top of the flight you'll need top and base rails, spindles and landing brackets. Some flights may require gooseneck rails, concave or convex ramps, horizontal turns or opening caps (see Options, p. 47), although these can be tricky to fit.

● Choose the type of wood for your new balustrade. Kits commonly offer a choice of light-colored hemlock or rich, dark Brazilian mahogany. These woods are best finished with varnish or polished to show off their grain and color, although you can apply a standard gloss paint system instead.

● Consider the local building code

Balustrade kits are easy to assemble, needing only modest carpentry skills.

CHECKLIST

Tools
power drill and bit
hole saw attachment
mallet
crosscut saw
compass saw
tape measure
level
try square
backsaw
surform tool (or spokeshave)
T-bevel or protractor
screwdriver
box wrench

Materials
stair components (newel bases, centers and caps, base and hand rails, brackets, spindles, spacer fillets), gap-filling resin
woodworking adhesive
sandpaper
nails

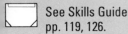 See Skills Guide pp. 119, 126.

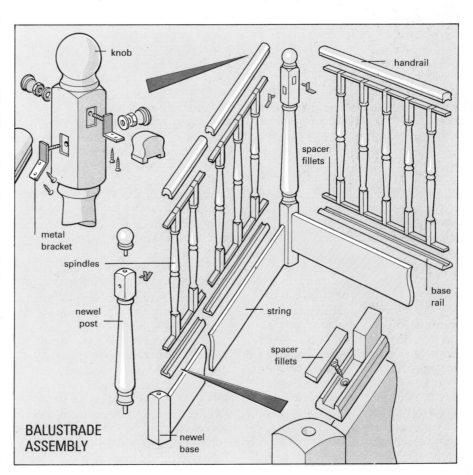

BALUSTRADE ASSEMBLY

knob — handrail — spacer fillets — metal bracket — spindles — newel post — string — spacer fillets — base rail — newel base

requirements regarding the safe design and construction of a staircase.

● Calculate the number of spindles and fillets you need. Count how many treads there are between the newels and allow two spindles per tread, although you'll only need one per tread where there's a cut-out for a newel post. To work out how many landing spindles you'll need measure the horizontal distance in inches then divide by 4.5. For example: $49\frac{1}{2} \div 4\frac{1}{2} = 11$ spindles. To calculate the number of fillets you'll need, double the number of spindles and add four.

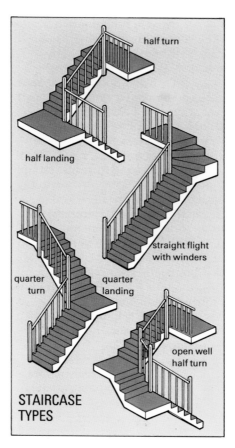

half turn

half landing

quarter turn

quarter landing

straight flight with winders

open well half turn

STAIRCASE TYPES

Identify your staircase type and make sure you know how the newel posts are fitted before starting

! **WATCH OUT FOR**

● newel posts that wobble when shaken. Constant use may have loosened the fixings at the base of the post on an old staircase. The newels are the main supporting posts of the balustrade and they may be bolted to underfloor joists or set in concrete. If your newel posts are fixed with bolts, check that the fixings aren't loose – tighten them if necessary with a socket or box wrench. If the newels are set in concrete fill in around the base of the post with mortar, working it well into the crack. Intermediate and top newels will be secured to the strings and upper floor joists; check and tighten these fixings if necessary.

● An open-string staircase, where the top edge of the string is cut to a stepped shape with the treads fixed on top. Normally the base of each spindle is housed in the tread and retained by a nosing, and this means you won't be able to use a base rail. Try to buy spindles which will fit in the existing housings. Alternatively, patch the housings and set the spindles on top of the treads, retaining them by skew

nailing, or with fillets.

● Side-fixed newel posts. Staircase kits rely on the newel being centered on the string, but with some flights the post is positioned to the outside of the inclined sides. You can't utilize the side-fixed post, so remove it and fit a newel base from the kit over the string, having marked out and cut a saddle joint in its lower end.

● Existing newels measuring less than $3\frac{1}{4}$in $\times$ $3\frac{1}{4}$in in cross-section, as cutting a hole for the center spigot would leave the 'walls' of the newel insufficiently thick. You may be able to manage with a newel $2\frac{3}{4}$in across so long as you build up the sides with cleats to a thickness of $3\frac{1}{4}$in.

● Cutting an off-center or slanted hole in the newel base for the newel center spigot – this would cause the completed balustrade to appear lopsided.

2 Remove old balustrade

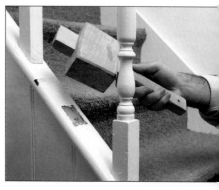

1. Use a wooden mallet to tap out the old skew-nailed spindles at the top and bottom

The first stage is to remove the existing balusters, rails or panelling between newel posts, and this depends on how the components are fixed.

If the balusters are skew-nailed to the hand rail you can simply tap them free with a mallet; if they're tenoned into the rail you'll have to saw through the tenons.

★ **TIP**

There may not be sufficient space to fit a crosscut saw between the balusters, so use a compass saw instead for the first few then change to the quicker crosscut saw when the gap is wide enough.

2. Saw through the handrail as close to the newel post as possible avoiding any metal brackets

3 Cut existing newel post

1. Cut through the newel post using a crosscut saw, taking great care that the saw cut is straight.

If your newel posts are center-fixed and of substantial enough section for reuse as bases, the next stage is to cut them down to size.

The lower newel base should be about 8in above the pitch line of the staircase. To find this point, place a straightedge across the nosings of two/three treads and mark the line of the slope.

Next, mark a horizontal line on the inside face of the post 8in up from the pitch line, using a try square. For a top newel post measure and square off 4¾in from the intersection; for an intermediate newel measure 7½in.

Cut through the wood at the marked point.

Lay a straightedge across the nosings to find the pitch line then cut 8in up the newel post

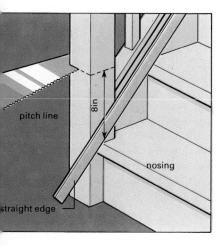

4 Fit the newel center

1. Drill out the center of the newel base to a depth of the spigot on the new newel post

2. Gouge out the wood from the hole, insuring that the sides are perfectly straight

The newel center has a spigot at the base, intended to fit into a large diameter hole bored in the top of the newel base. The hole must be cut accurately so that the spigot fits snugly and squarely. Determine the center of the base by drawing diagonal lines from the stub top's corners, then using a compass to draw a 2in diameter circle.

The easiest method of cutting the hole is to use a special hole saw attachment to a power drill which is fitted into the chuck. Drill the hole to the depth of the spigot in stages, clearing the debris as you go. If the hole saw won't drill deep enough you'll have to deepen the hole with a gouge.

Alternatively, drill a series of ¼in diameter holes just within the scribed circle to a depth of the spigot, then use a ¾in gouge to chisel out the waste wood, leaving the walls of the hole smooth.

Take the utmost care at each stage of the drilling and chiselling that the hole is straight, correcting any slight angle inside as soon as you spot it.

If the hole becomes too large, it's possible to pack it out with wedge shaped slivers of wood, but take great care when you fit the spigot that the fit is tight otherwise you may have a wobbly post.

Test-fit the newel center into the base but don't glue it yet. It is essential that the newel post is

3. Glue the spigot into the newel base hole, double checking with a level that it is straight

fitted centrally on the newel base and that it is perfectly vertical, otherwise there is a risk that your whole balustrade will be crooked. Use a level to check the position of the post before the glue has set and adjust if necessary by pulling gently. Repeat the operation for the top and intermediate newels.

★ TIP

For neatness and to insure a good fit it's preferable to chamfer the top face and four corners of the newel stub. Use a surform file or a spokeshave and finish off with sandpaper to remove any burrs from the stub.

5 Cut and fit the base rail

1. Use a T-bevel set along the string to find the angle of the staircase

The base rail must be marked and cut to length to match the angle of the staircase, then fixed to the top of the string.

Base rails usually come in standard lengths, and feature molded edges with a central channel to take the spindles and fillets. Before you can cut the rail to fit between the newels you have to find the pitch angle of the staircase. Use a T-bevel to determine this: hold the stock of the tool vertically against the newel base and adjust the blade to rest on top of the string. Tighten the nut to set the angle.

Transfer the angle to the side of the base rail, with the T-bevel's stock held up against the rail's

2. Transfer the angle from the T-bevel onto the base rail at the top and bottom

underside. Repeat for the other side of the rail then square lines across top and bottom using a try square.

Measure the distance between top and bottom newel bases, transfer to the base rail and scribe off at the other end with the T-bevel. Cut the base rail to length along the marked lines, taking care that you keep the sawn edges straight.

★ TIP

If you have a saber saw or circular saw with an adjustable sole plate, you can set this to produce the bevels required on the base rail, although you'll need to rig up a fence to guide the tool (see Skills Guide p. 125).

Drill clearance holes to take 1¼in flathead screws down the center of the base rail's channel, at about 12in intervals. Fit the rail over the string, align it and mark through the holes. Remove the rail, drill pilot holes in the string then return the rail and fix it in position by screwing through the predrilled holes.

If the existing newel base is the same size as the kit newel center, mark and cut the handrail to the same length and angle as the base rail, using the latter as a template. If it is smaller, the handrail must be shorter; if it is larger the hand rail must be longer.

3. Drill pilot holes in the base rail at regular intervals and screw it to the string

6 Assemble newels & rails

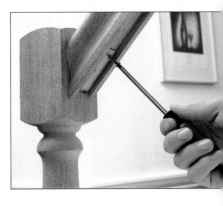

1. Screw the brackets onto the newel posts, slot the handrail on top then screw to the brackets

The newel posts and rails can now be fitted and connected, using the special metal brackets supplied with the balustrade kit.

Brackets comprise an angled flat section, pre-drilled with screw holes, with a threaded bolt welded onto the flange. The bolt slots through the newel centers and is secured at the other side by a washer and bolt.

★ TIP

So that the bracket flange will be flush with the end face of the handrail it's necessary to form a shallow hollow in the rail to house the weld on the back of the bracket.

Position the relevant bracket at each end of the handrail, mark and drill pilot holes then secure with the screws provided. Push the bolts through the holes in the newels, fit the washers and finger-tighten the nuts.

Apply adhesive to the top and bottom newel spigots and mount the post/rail assembly on the newel bases. Check that the newel posts are vertical using a level before tightening the bracket bolts fully with a socket or box wrench.

Glue the decorative wooden screw covers into the newels to conceal the bolts, then glue in the turned newel caps likewise.

7 Fit the spindles

1. Mark off the angle of the base rail on the first of the spindles using a T-bevel

2. Once you have marked one spindle, you can use it to mark the angle on the others

The spindles, or balusters, can now be cut to fit between hand and base rails and fixed in place using the pre-made spacer fillets.

The turned spindles have square ends which fit into the channels in the base and handrails, although they must be bevelled to match the angle of the string. First measure accurately between the bottom of the channels in both rails then cut one spindle to length, using your T-bevel or protractor to set the correct angle.

Place the spindle between the rails and check that it is vertical. Make any adjustments necessary then use the spindle as a template for cutting the remaining spindles.

The pre-cut fillets, which are bevel-ended to cope with different stair angles, are about 3½in long (the normal spindle spacing), although you can cut them down if you prefer.

Place the first two fillets in the base and handrails at the foot of the staircase and secure by dovetail nailing. Punch down the pin heads. Apply glue to the ends of the first spindle, position it in the channelling against the fillets and secure by skew-nailing. Fit another two fillets and another spindle, then repeat this procedure as you work up the staircase.

Where you're fitting spindles along a flat landing, trim the fillets

3. Fix the fillets into the base rail using glue and nails. Dovetail the nails in place

to length so that the spacing between balusters matches that on the stairs.

If your staircase is of the old-fashioned type without a string, the spindles should fit neatly into a housing on the stair tread. If the housing is too small, carefully enlarge it using a chisel. If it's too large, cut a small wedge shaped sliver of wood from a spare fillet, then glue and hammer it in place.

Finish off the completed balustrade by sealing the wood with a coat of polyurethane varnish thinned if necessary, followed by two or more coats of varnish, or by applying primer, undercoat and top coat of gloss.

8 Options

Less ornate, but rather graceful balustrades can be created using special handrail sections. The following examples of rail are designed to slot onto a peg in the top of a special newel post.

● **Start the handrail at the base of the flight with an opening cap and opening rise.**

● **A horizontal turn at a landing replaces a larger, ornate newel post.** If you'd prefer the smooth flow of the banister rail to be uninterrupted at a landing return, link with a right-angled section.

● **Connect lengths of hand rail using a tie bolt.** This is basically a woodscrew at one end with a machine thread and nut at the other. The screw is driven into the end of one section of rail, while the threaded part slots into a clearance hole drilled in the end of the meeting section. A large blind hole bored in the underside of the component gives access to the threaded end and enables a washer and bolt to be secured, using a box wrench, so locking the rail sections together. Always take your staircase measurements along to your supplier when buying the components so you can iron out any difficulties caused through extra long stairs before you start. ■

Beautiful balustrades can be created using the special handrail sections available

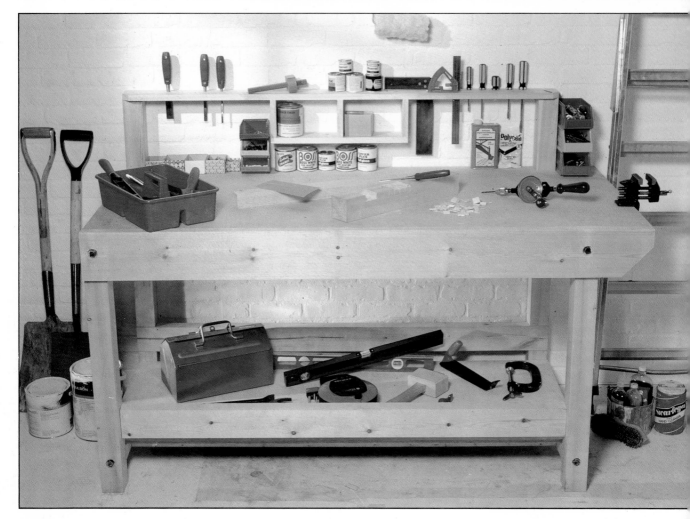

Do-it-Yourself Workbench

A sturdy workbench can be a real boon – this one is easy to make, adaptable, practical and cheaper than anything you'll find in the stores.

The construction of this tough and spacious workbench is simple: it's held together with basic housing and halving joints secured with screws and heavy-duty lag bolts. There's no need to use woodworking adhesive, so you can dismantle the parts without damaging them and reassemble the whole thing elsewhere.

Using the following assembly line illustrations it's an easy matter to adapt the length and depth to suit the spaces at your disposal – the only dimension that really matters is the height of the legs. And as you go through the steps of the assembly, there's ample opportunity to add extra features (like dividers and additional shelves) for yourself.

Apart from the ease of construction and dismantling, the bench features a spacious shelf for bulky tools and materials, a very sturdy top that will stand up to all sorts of abuses, and a handy tool rack.

CHECKLIST

Tools
crosscut saw and backsaw
saber saw
drill and bits
square and ruler
chisels and wrench

Materials
⅜in plywood
1in chipboard
Softwood:
   4 × 4, 2 × 3
   1 × 4, 2 × 4
   2 × 2, 2 × 6
   1 × 2
5in × ⅜in lag bolts
masonry bolts/assorted screws

See Skills Guide pp. 116, 118, 124, 129, 131.

WORKBENCH OPTIONS

Simple construction, but very robust, this workbench is made from two frames – front and back – tied together by softwood rails. Chipboard and plywood trays, and heavy-duty lag bolts hold it secure and a tool rack keeps things handy.

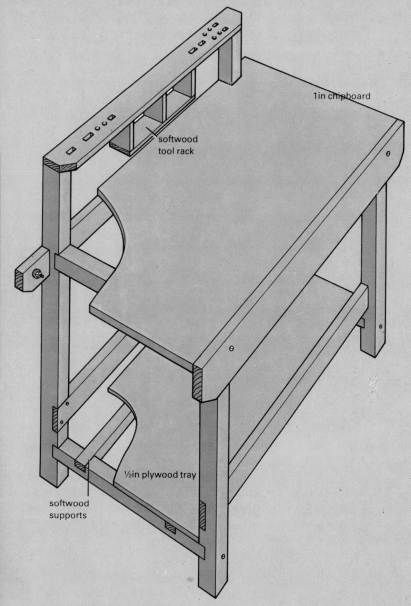

1in chipboard

softwood tool rack

½in plywood tray

softwood supports

The ideal height for a workbench is between 32in and 36in, determined here by the length of the legs and the thickness of the chipboard top. The overall length and depth is variable but, to make construction a little easier, limit the length to that of a standard sheet (8ft).

The chipboard top determines the overall length – it overhangs the frames to provide clamping surfaces at one or both ends. The rail at the top of the back frame is the same length – you can screw the rail overhang to the wall to provide extra rigidity. To dismantle, remove lag bolts.

PREPARE THE LEGS

The uprights are made from 4 × 4 softwood – you'll need to cut rabbets for the housing joints which hold the cross members and rails to the uprights. The long uprights form the rear legs of the workbench and also support the rear-mounted tool rack – you'll need to make two of each. Make the rear ones 1ft longer.

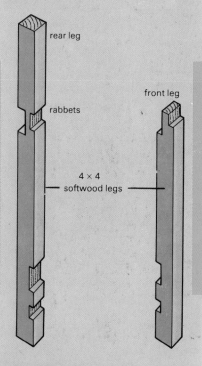

rear leg

rabbets

front leg

4 × 4 softwood legs

Cut housings to the full depth of the wall rail, ½in deep for others. Use one as a template for the others

Mark out the rabbets on the uprights, then cut down the sides with a backsaw. Remove the waste material with a sharp chisel – you'll find it easier if you saw a few extra cuts across the waste material first.

2 ASSEMBLE SIDE FRAMES

Once the legs are made, cut the halving joints on the long frame 1 × 4 – these fit into the rabbets in the legs and are secured by screws. Try to aim for a tight fit to eliminate movement – the more strength here the better. A temporary support 1 × 2 squares the front frame.

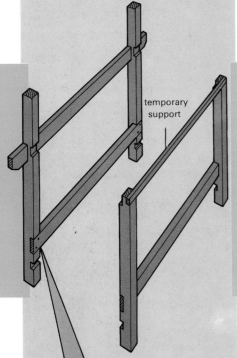

temporary support

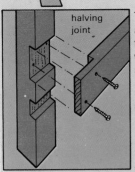

halving joint

The joints are held together with screws. Dry assemble for easy dismantling

Use screws to fit the halving joints loosely, check the two frames against each other to make sure that they are the same size and shape and that they are square. Tighten up the screws once the frames are set correctly.

3 MAKE THE BOTTOM SHELF

Nail the shelf to the 2 × 2 framing once it is square

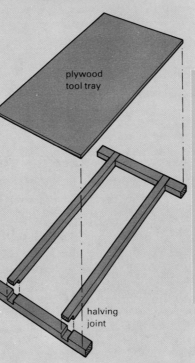

plywood tool tray

halving joint

The bottom shelf is a sheet of ⅜in plywood supported by 2 × 3 and 2 × 2 softwood framing. The joints only need to be held with single screws as the frame is held square by the plywood shelf secured by nails. Cut the halving joints in the softwood framing in the same way as the legs and longitudinal bracing. Make sure that you hold the frame absolutely square as you nail the tray into place as you won't get another chance to correct it without pulling all the nails out. Dovetail nailing is the best technique for holding sheet to bearers once the first few corner nails are in.

4 ASSEMBLE THE MAIN FRAME

Until you secure the lag bolts, the assembled frame will be unstable. The 5in lag bolts, followed by the chipboard top, secure the parts. Make sure that you keep the cross-members square to the side frames as you drill the clearance holes for each lag bolt. Nail down the center brace.

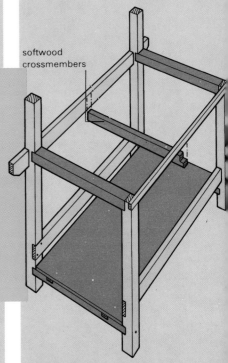

softwood crossmembers

Check for square and clamp the parts as you drill holes for the lag bolts. Holes must be absolute square to the legs

The side frames are held in place by the bottom shelf assembly and by 2 × 3 cross-members. All joints are dry housings. Lag bolts through the legs drive into the end grains of the cross members

FIT THE BENCH TOP

The top should end up flush with the front edge of the frame. Attach the top to the frame parts with 2in No. 10 flathead screws at approximately 4in intervals around the frame dimensions. Secure in the same way to the center brace. Once fitted, the bench will suddenly feel very robust.

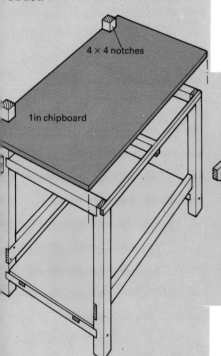

4 × 4 notches

1in chipboard

Cut the 1in board to the length of the wall rail and the full depth. Use a saber saw to cut notches for the tool rack

'Direct measure' the bench top – it must be the length of the wall rail on the back frame and the total depth of the main frame. Use a saber saw to cut notches in the top so that it will fit neatly around the tool rack 'legs'.

FIT THE FRONT LIP

Counter bore the lag bolts and tighten with a wrench to complete the frame

front member

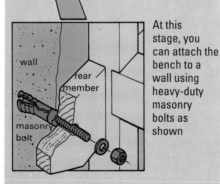

wall

rear member

masonry bolt

At this stage, you can attach the bench to a wall using heavy-duty masonry bolts as shown

Use 2 × 6 softwood (or similar) for the heavy-duty front lip. Cut it to the length of the bench top. Complete the frame assembly by securing the lag bolts through the lip and legs and into the cross-members.

ADD THE TOOL RACK

Make the tool rack from 1 × 4 softwood. Cut holes for your tools using a drill or chisel

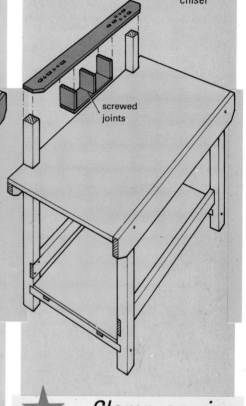

screwed joints

Clamp-on vise

Sometimes a permanently-fixed vise gets in the way of your working area. An inexpensive clamp-on vise need not.

CHECKLIST

Materials
1½ sheets of ⅝in and ½ sheet of ¼in birch-faced plywood
25ft of ½in quarter-round beading
¼in fluted dowels
flush-door hinges
magnetic catches
flap/door stays
½in and 1in brads
PVA adhesive
sandpaper
handles as required

Tools
saber saw or circular saw
fine crosscut saw
backsaw
plane
try square
dowel jig
hammer
coping saw
tape measure, ruler
drill and assorted bits
screwdriver, bradawl
marking gauge

See Skills Guide
pp. 113, 116, 122, 128

Modular Storage Units

These stacking units make an ideal storage and display medium in any number of situations. They're modular and adaptable – you can fit and finish any number together, upright or horizontally.

Lack of display shelves and units is an obvious problem in many homes, and most rooms could do with combined storage and display space for all those things you want at hand but not under your feet.

This modular system of storage gets around the problem by rationalising the space available – you can make as many units as you want for a combination of storage and display, you can put doors on or leave them off, you can add drawers, you can stack the units or make them larger – as long as you change the

cutting list accordingly.

The units are very easy to build – they're rectangular boxes held together with dowels and glue instead of complicated joints. You can alter the design shown here to suit any room or fit any space or to match the size of the items to be stored and displayed. One attractive feature is that doors and shelves are set back from the leading edges so you'll have to use cranked cabinet hinges; otherwise, the choice of hardware is up to you.

If you've got enough storage

space inside, units like these w come in equally handy outside in th shop or garage, where good storag space is always in short suppl You'll then be able to use a cheap material as appearance wor matter so much.

The best material to make th units from is plywood, suitab stained and varnished. If you wa to incorporate drawers make the from softwood or plywood and tri the front with veneered plywoo Choose handles to match the rest the unit. See Skills Guide pp. 11 116, 122, 128 to help you cut the u panels and fit them together.

THE BASIC UNIT

The simplest module has two top-to-bottom sides, fitted with four shelves and a ⅛in backing panel. Divide the sides into three for the same shelf spacing on all modules. All shelves are 1¼in smaller all around than the width of the sides to allow for the ⅝in thickness of the material and to set them back from the leading front edge by a uniform amount

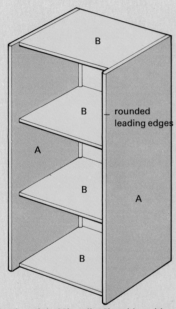

rounded leading edges

A basic unit is 32in tall, 16in wide, with shelves 14¾in deep

DESIGN OPTIONS

If you want to combine storage with display shelves, you can fit the basic unit with doors or drawers or both. You'll need extra material, handles, hinges and catches. The main carcase is identical to the basic module and with the same proportions. You can make all three versions from 1½ full sheets of ⅝in plywood

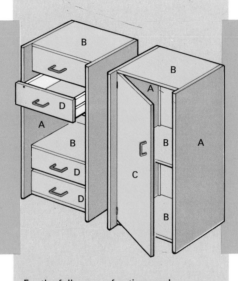

For the full range of options and combinations, make one basic, one drawer and one cupboard unit

MAKE A CUTTING LIST

To make three units of the same size in different styles, mark out 1½ full sheets 8ft × 4ft as shown. Note that B, C and D are smaller – you must allow for the thickness of the material (⅝in) if you want to stack units – remove a 3⅝in margin and divide what remains into three. See Skills Guide pp. 118

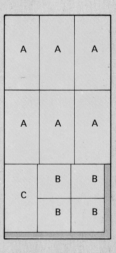

The job will be much easier using a power saw, unless your supplier will cut it for you (give your supplier a cutting list first)

Bevel the leading edges of all pieces of A after cutting. Work from the edges to avoid splitting or splintering the ends. See Skills Guide p. 122

★ *Using modular units*

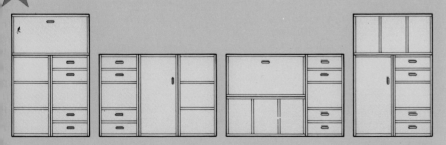

Because they're modular, you can use the units in any of the combinations shown above – the width of two is the same as the height (or length) of one. Basic units can be used horizontally or vertically but drawer units can only be

vertical. If you want to fit doors with flush-door hinges, you can use the unit as a cupboard or, if fitted with cabinet stays, as a low bureau. If you want to change sizes, make a cutting list to keep the dimensions modular (see above).

PREPARE THE COMPONENTS

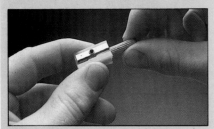

Use a pencil sharpener to round off
the ends of the dowels slightly

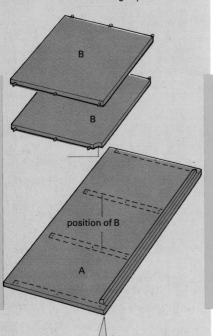

*Mark the edges of the shelves for
fitting dowels. You'll need three per
shelf – one 2in in front each edge and
one in the center (see right). Divide
each side (A) into three and drill them
for their dowels too. You'll also need to
fit quarter-round to the sides to accept
the back panel. If the back panel is to sit
against the shelves, you must notch the
back corners of the shelves to fit
around it*

FIT THE SHELVES

With the shelves cut and fitted with dowels,
glue and attach the side panel (A)

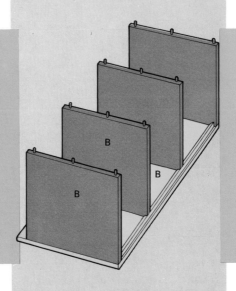

*All four shelves are dowel-jointed and
the two middle shelves must have
notches cut from the rear corners to
clear the quarter-round*

COMPLETE THE BOX

*Place one side (A) on a flat surface,
then glue and attach all four shelves.
Glue and attach the second side (see
left). Make sure the sides are the right
way around and that the molding fits
into the shelf notches. You may have to
tap the sides to get the dowels fully
home. Clamp the box together to dry
using bar clamps or a string or band
clamp, see Skills Guide. Check the box
remains square as it dries. If you prefer,
nail a thin bracing cleat across the
diagonal length.*

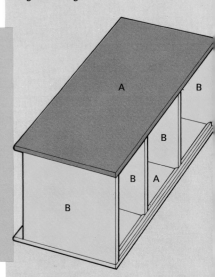

*Assemble the unit dry to check the fit
and adjust as necessary. Glue all the
mating edges and re-assemble, then
clamp tight and allow the glue to dry*

ATTACH THE BACK PANEL

Cut an inset back banel from ⅛in hardboard using a backsaw

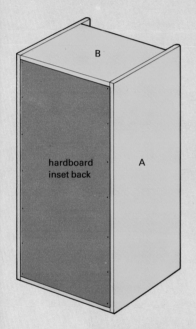

FIT THE DRAWERS

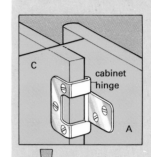

For drawer units, attach the runners before final assembly.

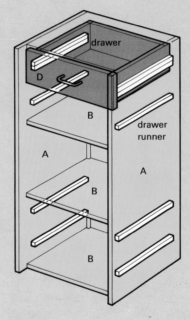

HANG THE DOORS

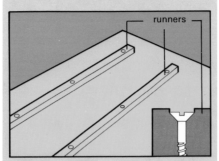

Flush door hinges enable recessed doors to clear the sides of the unit

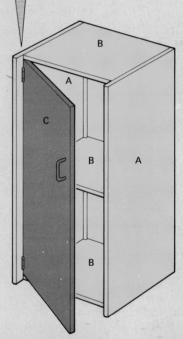

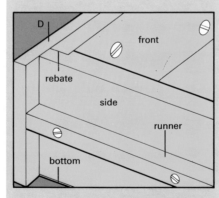

Glue and brad the back panel to the quarter-round and to the back edges of the shelves. The back panel is not just for decorative effect – it adds to the stability of the unit and helps to keep it square

It's easiest to use complete drawer kits made from plastic sections. Attach plywood fronts: the depth of the drawer front should be half the distance between the shelves with a ⅛in clearance

To make a truly versatile combination, fit check straps to the door so that the unit can be used vertically or horizontally whenever you choose, there's a choice of plastic or metal straps available or use metal stays

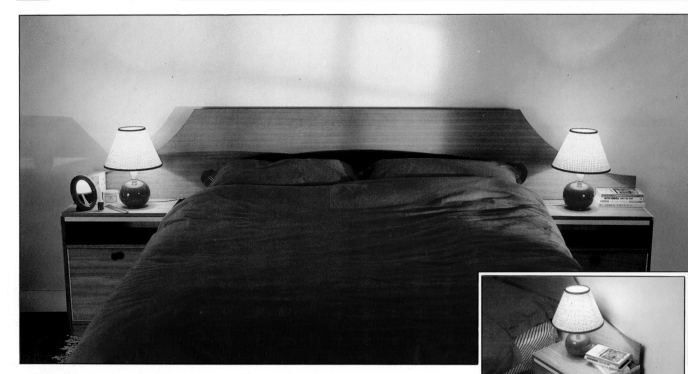

Unique Headboard Unit

This made-to-measure headboard unit has visual and very practical appeal – the headboard offers support and the cabinets provide bedside storage.

A bed without a headboard seems strangely naked and if you don't have a cupboard or table beside the bed, the alarm clock and other odds and ends inevitably get dumped on the floor.

This design for a complete headboard unit solves these problems: it incorporates a pair of useful bedside cupboards as well as a full-size headboard. You could even have the headboard upholstered for greater comfort.

The design can be tailored to suit your needs and it can be adapted to fit around a single or double bed. The unit is made from veneered plywood which is readily available in standard sheets – you can save time by taking a cutting list to your lumber yard and get them to saw the sheets up for you.

The headboard for the illustrated unit was cut from a sheet 15in wide; the shelves and tops from two sheets 12in wide; and the back panels from a sheet 18in wide. All the sheets were 8ft long. You can cut out the panels with a crosscut saw but it will be much easier if you use a saber saw.

Although the cabinet doors in the featured unit are hinged at the bottom so that they open downwards, there is no reason why you can't side-hinge them if you prefer.

All the panels which go to make up the cabinets are held together with square-section cleats that are secured with screws. As some of these cleats are left exposed to become a visually important part of the design, it's a good idea if they are cut from an attractive hardwood like maple. The exposed cleats are matched with strips of molding which trim the doors and top panel.

HEADBOARD AND BEDSIDE CABINETS COMBINED

The headboard straddles the gap between the two cabinets and is braced by concealed offcuts of plywood (G1). To add interest to the design, it's a good idea to shape the ends; they can be scalloped (as shown), rounded or fashioned into more elaborate forms with a saber saw or coping by hand with a saw.

There are several options open to you when it comes to the cabinets. The doors can be either side or bottom hinged, or they can be omitted altogether. A further option is to 'shape' the cabinets (bottom) and there is no reason why you can't add more shelves or fit adjustable shelves on shelf pins

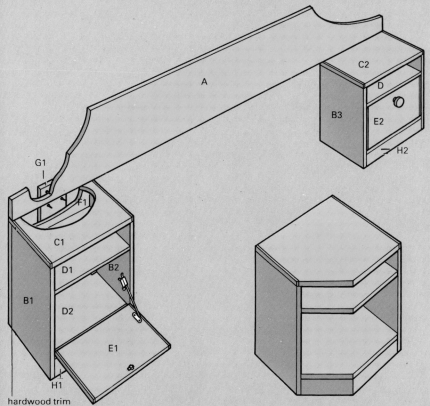

hardwood trim

The length of the headboard should equal the width of the bed plus the combined widths of the two bedside cabinets. Within reason, the cabinets can be as wide and as deep as you like – 18in × 12in are well proportioned dimensions.

The height of the cabinets (and consequently the headboard) will depend on the distance between bed and floor. Generally speaking, it's best to make the top of the cabinets level with the top of the mattress for greatest comfort and convenience.

The sides of the top pieces (C) and the doors (E) are trimmed with hardwood strips – you must make allowances for the thicknesses of these strips when you work out your cutting list (see Skills Guide p. 113). Choose a wood color and grain to complement the veneered plywood – use the same wood for shelf support cleats and trims.

When you have assembled the whole unit, apply at least three coats of varnish, not forgetting to sand down each coat lightly once it has dried.

CUT OUT THE PANELS

Score along your cutting lines with a knife to avoid ragged saw cuts

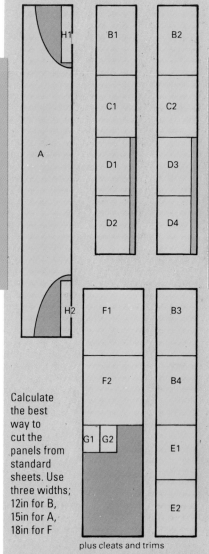

Calculate the best way to cut the panels from standard sheets. Use three widths; 12in for B, 15in for A, 18in for F

plus cleats and trims

Mark out and label all the panels before sawing. Use a card template to describe curves on the headboard. Waste on shelves (D) is the thickness of the backs (F). H, D are equal lengths

FIX THE CLEATS

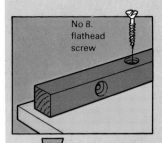

No 8. flathead screw

Sink all screw heads into the wood

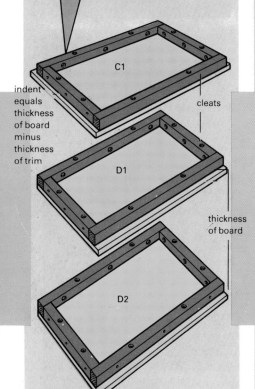

indent equals thickness of board minus thickness of trim

C1

cleats

D1

thickness of board

D2

Align cleats, then start screw holes in the panels with a bradawl

The square-section cleats act as jointing blocks for the various panels. Be sure to position each one accurately, especially when it is set back from the edge

ADD THE BACK PANELS

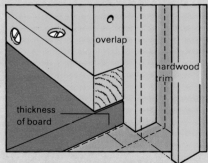

overlap

hardwood trim

thickness of board

The overlap, combined with the trim, equals the board thickness

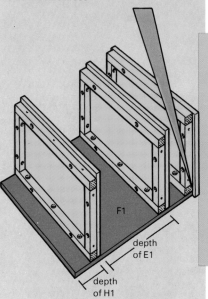

F1

depth of E1

depth of H1

Use glue, as well as screws, to fix the shelves

Starting from the bottom, scribe lines across the back panel to mark the positions of the shelves. Use a plinth (H1) to help line up the lower shelf, and a door for the middle one

ATTACH THE SIDES

The shelves must be parallel with the top

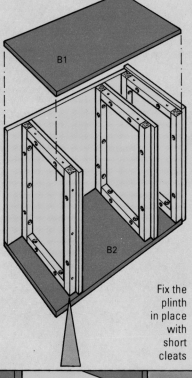

B1

B2

Fix the plinth in place with short cleats

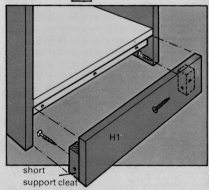

H1

short support cleat

You will find it easier to screw into the side panels if you lay them on a flat work surface. Square lines across the boards to align the shelves

TRIM THE EDGES

Trim the top and door panels with hardwood strips

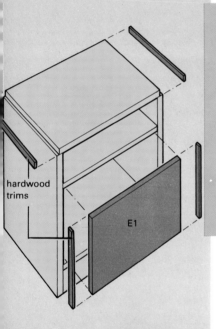

hardwood trims

E1

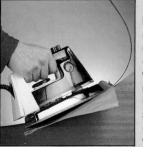

Finish off other edges with matching iron-on or self-stick edging veneer

Finish off the exposed edges of plywood with strips of maple and lengths of iron-on edging veneer. Sink all the brad heads below the surface of the wood using a nailset

ADD THE HARDWARE

Cut piano hinges to length with a hacksaw

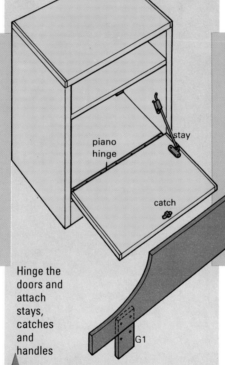

piano hinge

stay

catch

Hinge the doors and attach stays, catches and handles

G1

ATTACH THE HEADBOARD

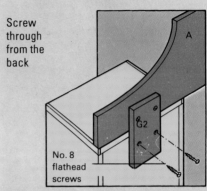

Screw through from the back

A

G2

No. 8 flathead screws

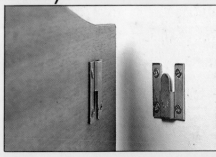

handle

The bottom edge of the headboard rests on top of the cabinets; its ends should be flush with the sides. Secure the headboard with offcuts

★ *Wall-mounting made easy*

Flushmount Fittings *provide an excellent way of mounting the headboard (without the cabinets) on a wall*

The fittings comprise *two halves which interlock with each other. Spaced accordingly, they make a concealed, but lift-off attachment*

59

Go-Anywhere Cabinet

Inexpensive, easy to make and easy to adapt to the size you need, this simple design for a cabinet-on-castors belies its usefulness – it's a multi-purpose item with a home in any room.

There's room in every home for this combination storage and display cabinet. You can adapt it to suit a specific purpose – just vary the dimensions indicated to suit your needs – or you can build it to the optimum sizes shown on the follow-ing pages and just use it for all sorts of jobs. You'll have no trouble moving it from room to room – hidden castors make it a go-anywhere cabinet.

Hi-fi companion? Simply slot in the equipment, plug it in and park it next to your favorite chair. Bedside table? There's room for a coffee cup, a lamp and all your bedside reading matter, yet you can move it aside in a second for easy bed-making. Telephone stand? It will accommo-date even the fanciest phone, a message pad and a pile of phone books. Use off-the-shelf planks of veneered or plastic-coated chip-board and there's little cutting and hardly any finishing.

CHECKLIST

Tools
try or combination square
marking knife or pencil
tape measure
crosscut saw or saber saw
hand or power drill
sandpaper on sanding block
screwdriver
chisel or coping saw
mini hacksaw
straightedge
electric iron

Materials
veneered plywood
self-stick trim
joint blocks
plate-fixing castors
piano hinge
door knobs and catches
plug-in shelf supports
flathead screws/brads
polyurethane varnish

See Skills Guide pp. 113–6, 125, 133.

1

MARK OUT THE COMPONENTS

The sizes for the cabinet are:

A 26in × 12in   **E** 18in × 4½in
B 18in × 8in   **F** 18in × 2½in
C 18in × 10½in   **G** 13in × 9in
D 18in × 12in   **H** 17⅞in × 10in

The inset masonite back is 19¼in × 18⅛in. All can be cut from two planks.

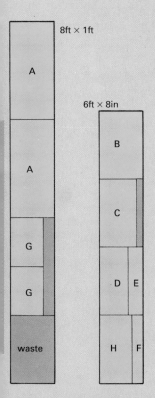

8ft × 1ft

A

A

G

G

waste

6ft × 8in

B

C

D   E

H   F

Use a saber saw to cut all the pieces to size

Mark out and label all the components on the planks, then cut them to length. If you use a saber saw for this, clamp a 1 × 2 across the plank at each cutting line to act as a guide.

2

REMOVE THE CUT-OUTS

Use a try square to mark the outline of the rear cut-out; this should measure about 2⅝in × 2in.

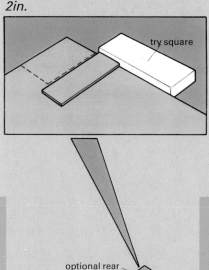

try square

optional rear cut-out

A

combination square

Mark out the rectangular rear and triangular front cut-outs carefully. The front one is a triangle with sides measuring 5in. Then cut each one carefully and sand the cut edges.

3

MARK THE SHELF POSITIONS

Mark out all the shelf positions on both side pieces with a long straightedge

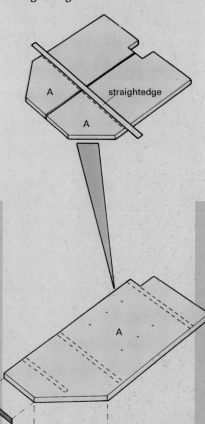

A

A

straightedge

A

edge veneer

Trim the edge veneer with a special cutter or a sanding block

To insure accurate alignment of the shelves, lay both parts **A** side by side and mark the shelf and shelf support positions using a straightedge. Glue edge veneer on the top of **A** and trim.

4

ATTACH THE JOINT BLOCKS

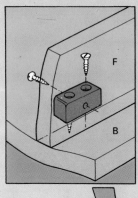

Screw joint blocks to the underside of each fixed shelf end and add one inset along the rear edge of **B** to support the rear upright **E**

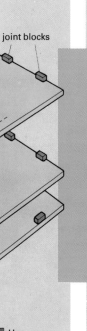

cut-out for cord

joint blocks

B

C or D

E

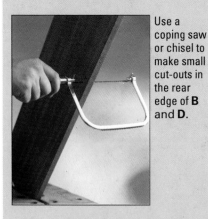

Use a coping saw or chisel to make small cut-outs in the rear edge of **B** and **D**.

*The simplest assembly method is to use small joint blocks, screwed to the underside of each shelf end. For hi-fi or a phone, make cord cut-outs in **B** and **D**.*

5

ASSEMBLE THE CARCASE

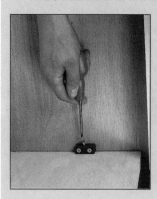

Position each shelf to the marked line on the side panels and drive in the screw

A

D

B

A

*Make up the main carcase of the cart by linking parts **A**, **B** and **D** using joint blocks, and checking for square.*

6

ADD THE INSET BACK

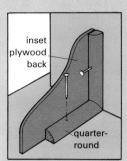

inset plywood back

quarter-round

Screw small magnetic catches to the front edge of shelf **B**

position of C

*Cut the inset back panel from ⅛in hardboard and glue it to the lengths of quarter-round tacked to **A**, **B** and **D**.*

▼7
FIT THE MIDDLE SHELF

*Make a rounded cut-out in each rear corner of shelf **C** so it will fit flush against the cabinet back*

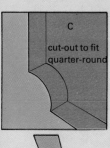

C

cut-out to fit quarter-round

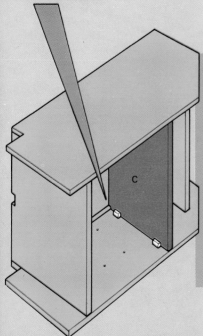

C

Drive brads in through the back into the molding and the rear edge of shelf **C**

*Slide shelf **C** into position, lining its edges up with the pencil lines drawn in step 3, and put it in place with four joint blocks. Use an offcut of molding to mark the small cutouts in the rear corners.*

▼8
COMPLETE THE CARCASE

Attach the rear upright **E** to the underside of the rear edge of **B** using the joint blocks attached in stage 4

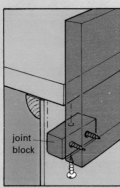

joint block

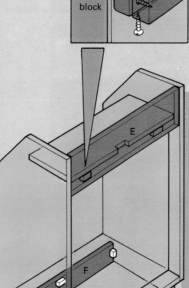

E

F

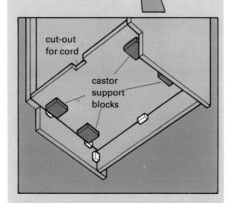

cut-out for cord

castor support blocks

*Attach the rear upright **E** and the plinth **F**, then screw on four ⅝in thick castor supports.*

▼9
HANG THE DOORS

Screw small magnetic catches to the front edge of shelf. **B**

screw-in knobs

G   G

piano hinge

H

shelf studs

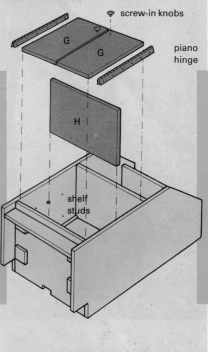

Attach the castor plates to the support blocks and press in the castors

*Complete the cabinet by hanging the doors using two lengths of piano hinge, and fit each with a small screw-on knob. Then fit the castors, slide in shelf **H** and finish the unit with varnish.*

Made-To-Measure Cart

Every home has its storage problems – awkward corners that off-the-shelf units won't fill but random junk always will. A cart made to fit the available space is the perfect answer

Most modern kitchens end up with a narrow space between units and appliances that nothing in the catalogs will fit. In bathrooms, there's often a gap left between the head of the bath and the wall that's simply boxed in and wasted. And under the stairs is probably the worst place of all to make sensible use of – it's either paneled in and full of hidden mysteries, or open-plan and colonized by abandoned boots and shoes, footballs and old magazines.

This easy-to-make mobile cart can be adapted in shape and size to suit all these spaces – and similar ones you may have in children's rooms, utility rooms and so on. All you need to do is take measurements of the gap it's got to fill and work out your cutting list to match. The instructions that follow tell you everything else you need to know.

CHECKLIST

Tools
try square
marking knife or pencil
tape measure
fine crosscut saw or sabersaw
hand or power drill + bits
screwdriver
electric iron

Optional extras
trimmer for iron-on edging
long straightedge
small C-clamps + 1×2

Materials
planks of plastic-coated
or veneered plywood
iron-on edging
joint blocks
plate-fixing castors
plug-in shelf supports
1in No. 8 flathead screws
1½in No. 8 flathead screws
handle(s) to taste

See Skills Guide
pp. 113–5

A

BATHROOM/KITCHEN UNIT

This square-ended unit will fit into a recess of almost any shape or size in a bathroom or kitchen. In the bathroom the top can be tiled to match the color of the bathroom fixtures; in a kitchen the top can be omitted and the exposed end of the unit finished to match the existing kitchen unit doors. Leave out the adjustable shelves if you want to store tall items.

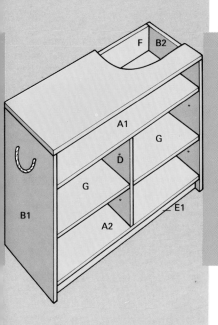

Working out your cutting list

Measure up the recess the unit will fit. Then subtract 1in from each measurement to give the unit's overall height (H), width (W) and depth (D).

Skills Guide p. 113 explains how to work out a detailed cutting list like the one below.

Detailed cutting list

Plinth height is (P), shelf spacing is (S), board thickness is (T). Measure height (H), width (W) and depth (D).

Sides A are (H minus T)in by (D)in = ( )×( )in

Top B is (W)in by (D)in = ( ) × ( )in

Shelves C are (W minus 2T) in by (D minus T)in = ( )×( )in

B

UNDERSTAIRS UNITS

The ends of the understairs units are angled to match the slope of the staircase. You can make just one unit, or a complete nest to fill the understairs triangle. All are assembled in the same way as the bathroom unit, with the large unit having an extra shelf and the small one just a bottom shelf. Again, the adjustable shelves are optional.

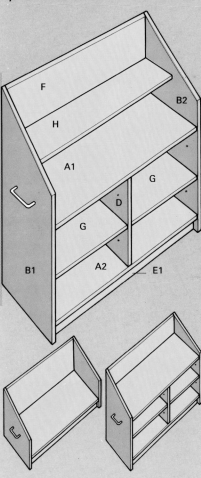

Divider D is (2S plus T)in by (D minus T)in = ( ) × ( )

Plinths E are (W minus 2T)in by (P)in = ( ) × ( )in

Back F is (W minus 2T)in by (H minus T minus P)in = ( ) × ( )in

Shelves G are ½(W minus 3T)in by (D minus T)in = ( ) × ( )in

Shelf H is (W minus 2T)in by ¾(D)in = ( ) × ( )in

1

MARK OUT THE COMPONENTS

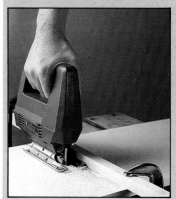

Use a straight edge clamped to the board as a cutting guide

Typical cutting plan

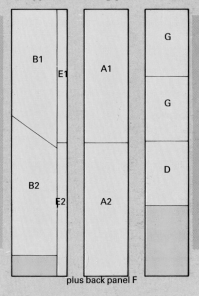

plus back panel F

Stick edge trim to the cut edges of the boards

Mark out, cut and label all the components. Whether you're working with planks or full-sized boards, work out the most economical arrangement first. See Skills Guide pp. 113–4

MARK THE SHELF POSITIONS

Use tape on the drill as a depth guide for the shelf support sockets

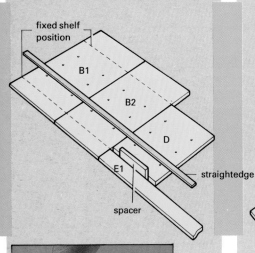

fixed shelf position

straightedge

spacer

Trim off the overlap of the edging with a sharp knife or special trimmer

Align the sides and central divider plus a plinth and a spacer to allow for the bottom shelf. Mark the fixed and adjustable shelf positions across all three at once using a long straightedge

ASSEMBLE THE CARCASE

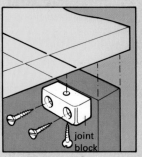

Attach joint blocks to the shelves first, then to the sides. Use two at each end of the shelf

joint block

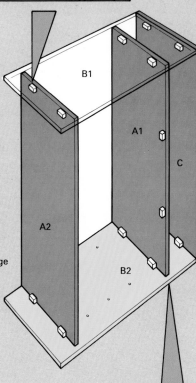

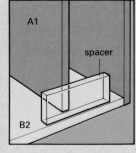

Use an offcut of the board as a spacer to inset the shelves (C) and allow for the inset back panel

spacer

Begin to assemble the carcase by linking the two sides with the top and bottom shelf. Then add the middle shelf. Align each shelf with the pencil lines marked in step 2. See Skills Guide p. 115

ADD THE CENTRAL DIVIDER

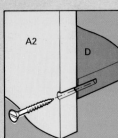

Drive screws up through the bottom shelf into the central divider to secure it invisibly in place

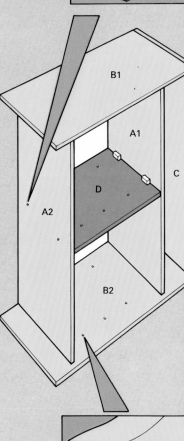

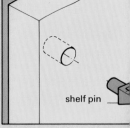

Insert the shelf support pins in the pre-drilled holes in the sides and divider

shelf pin

Fit the central divider with joint blocks at the top, flathead screws at the bottom. It's easier to lay the unit on its back to drill the pilot holes through a center line and drive in the screws

COMPLETE THE CARCASE

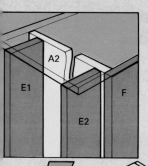

Inset the plinths by about 1in front and back, and secure them with joint blocks

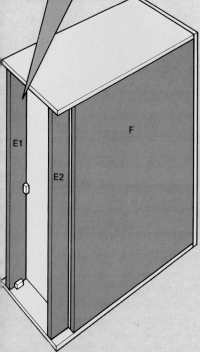

Attach joint blocks to the back and screw through them into the top, sides and bottom shelf to complete the carcase. Add the plinths at the front and back

ATTACH THE CASTORS

Screw the castor plates to the blocks and press each castor into position

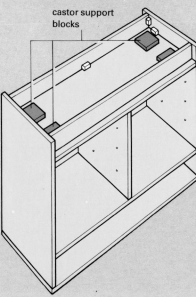

castor support blocks

Screw castor support blocks made from offcuts to the underside of the bottom shelf so the castors lift the unit about ¼in clear of the floor

ADD THE HANDLES

Drill holes to match the fixing centers of bar handles and secure the handles on the inside with washers and nuts

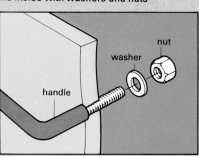

nut

washer

handle

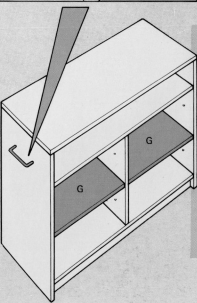

G

G

Finish off each cabinet with handles so you can pull them in and out easily. Use nylon rope instead of bar handles if you wish (knot the ends inside)

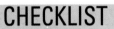

Fold-up Cart

If you're tired of hurrying from the kitchen loaded with food and drinks, and yet lack the space for a traditional serving cart, this sleek, fold-away model is exactly what you need. And you don't have to be a master craftsman to make it.

This fold-away serving cart is specially designed to be functional as well as good-looking. Its shelves are staggered to make it easy to reach every corner, and hinged, so that when the cart is not in use you can slide them forwards to lie flat

against the framework, giving a compact easily stored unit.

Making the cart is straightforward. The trickiest part of the job is forming the halving joints that connect the pieces of the framework together. Provided you take care to mark and cut these accurately, the rest of the construction is simple.

The illustrated cart is finished by coloring the wood with black stain. This emphasizes the wood's grain, and contrasts dramatically with the stark, white laminate. Of course, you can vary the effect with other color combinations, or use paint or varnish instead.

CHECKLIST

Materials
Softwood: 40ft × 1in × 2in,
5ft × 1in × 1in
½in plywood
½in dowelling
1½in × ½in butt hinges
1¼in flathead screws
½in quarter-round
PVA and contact adhesive
wood stain, paint or varnish
castors
laminate
contact adhesive

Tools
screwdriver
backsaw
miter box
tape measure
½in bevel edged chisel
laminate cutter
try square
C-clamps
drill and ½in dowelling bit

See Skills Guide pp. 113, 116, 118, 128–30, 132.

THE CART'S DESIGN

The main framework of the cart, made exclusively from 1 × 2, comprises two ladder-like frames which are hinged together at the top. The shelves – sheets of laminate-clad plywood with wooden edging – are hinged to cleats (G) attached to the main framework.

Two small wooden stops glued to the underside of the shelves locate with short dowels in the cross members (C) and hold the shelves open when the cart is erect.

When not in use the folded cart can rest unobtrusively against a wall or you can hang it from its handle on a hook.

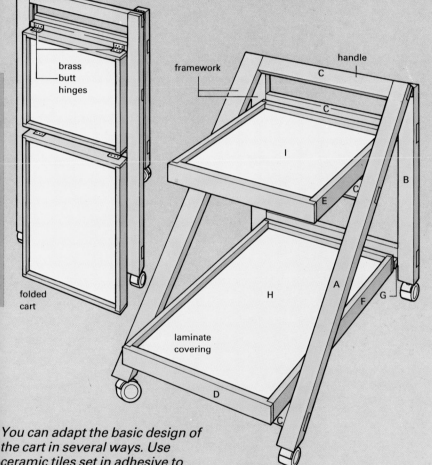

brass
butt
hinges

framework

handle

C
C
I
C
B
E
A
F
G
H
D
C

folded cart

laminate covering

You can adapt the basic design of the cart in several ways. Use ceramic tiles set in adhesive to cover the shelves (right). For a neat professional finish, fix extra molding around the top edges of the shelves to stop crumbs from collecting and round off the handle with a surform tool.

The lumber sizes specified here make a cart large enough for most household uses, but if you want to vary the size, reduce all the pieces proportionately using scale drawing.

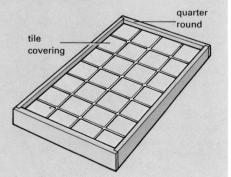

quarter round

tile covering

CUT THE COMPONENTS

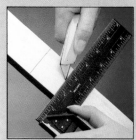

Cut the framework pieces squarely using a knife and try square to mark them first

A = 46in
B = 31½in
C = 25½in
D = 21½in
E = 19in
F = 30¾in
G = 21½in

A (×2)
B (×2)
C (×5)
D (×4)
E (×2)
F (×2)
G (×2)

H

I

H = 29¾in × 20in
I = 18in × 20in

Smooth the rough edges of the plywood with a sanding block

Mark and cut the required number of parts A, B, C, D, E and F from 1 × 2in softwood, then cut parts G and two 7in stop cleats from 1 × 1in wood. Use a miter box to make sure you cut squarely. Cut the shelves (H and I) from a sheet of ½in plywood.

MAKE THE FRAMES

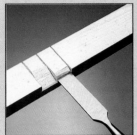

Mark out the halving joints then cut down the depth lines with a backsaw. Remove the waste with a sharp chisel

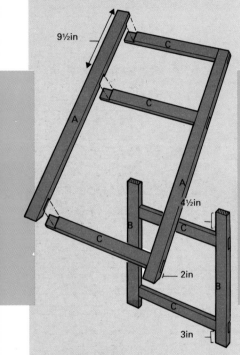

9½in

A

A

4½in

B

C

C

2in

B

C

3in

Apply glue to one component of each joint. Assemble the framework and clamp the joints until the adhesive has set

Cut a 45 degree miter at one end of both parts A, then make halving joints (see Skills Guide p. 129) 2in in from the mitered ends and 9½in in from the others. Cut corner halving joints at both ends of each part C, and at the unmitered ends of parts A. Check that the pieces fit, then glue them.

COVER THE SHELVES

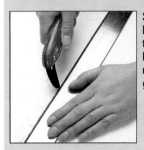

Score the laminate along the marked lines, using a metal rule as a guide

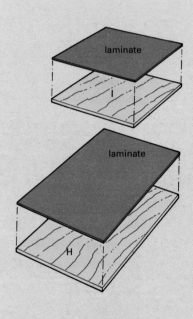

laminate

I

laminate

H

Spread contact adhesive on the mating surfaces and when touch dry, position the laminate

Outline the shelves (H and I) on a sheet of laminate, then score along the marked lines with a laminate cutter. Apply contact adhesive to the laminate and the shelves. After about 15 minutes set the laminate in place and cover with a weight until the adhesive sets (see Skills Guide).

FRAME THE SHELVES

Use a back-saw to cut 45 degree miters at the ends of the quarter-round

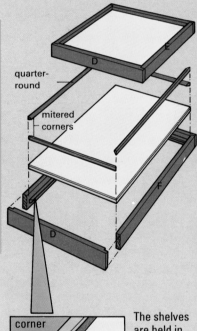

E

D

quarter-round

mitered corners

F

D

corner halving joint

The shelves are held in place by strips of molding above and below

Cut corner halving joints at both ends of the front and back shelf framing pieces (D). Use them to connect the frame side pieces (E and F), making rectangular frames for the shelves. Tack and glue lengths of beading (with 45° miters) to the frames, trapping the shelves in place.

ASSEMBLE THE CART

Join the front and back frames with hinges attached spine upwards

butt hinge

C A B

Screw cleats to the back frame crosspieces; attach the shelves to these with hinges placed spine down

C G B

Attach hinges to the front and back frame side pieces (A and B), flush with the tops, and with their spines facing up. Screw cleats (G) to the back frame cross-pieces (C), flush with the lower edges. Fit the shelve to the cleats.

FIT SHELF STOPS

Open up the cart and mark the stop positions underneath the shelves

90°

1in × 1in cleat

locating hole

½in dowel

Attach the stops to the shelves and the dowels to the frame using woodworking adhesive

Make a ½in hole through the middle of each shelf stop. Drill holes in the front frame crosspieces to take vertical dowels. Fit the dowels then sit the stops on top. When the shelves are horizontal, attach the stops.

FINISH THE CART

Screw the castors into the underside of the front and back frame legs

castors

Attach castors to the front and back cart frames by screwing them into the undersides of the frame legs (A and B). Finish the trolley by coating the wood with paint, varnish, or, as here, colored wood stain.

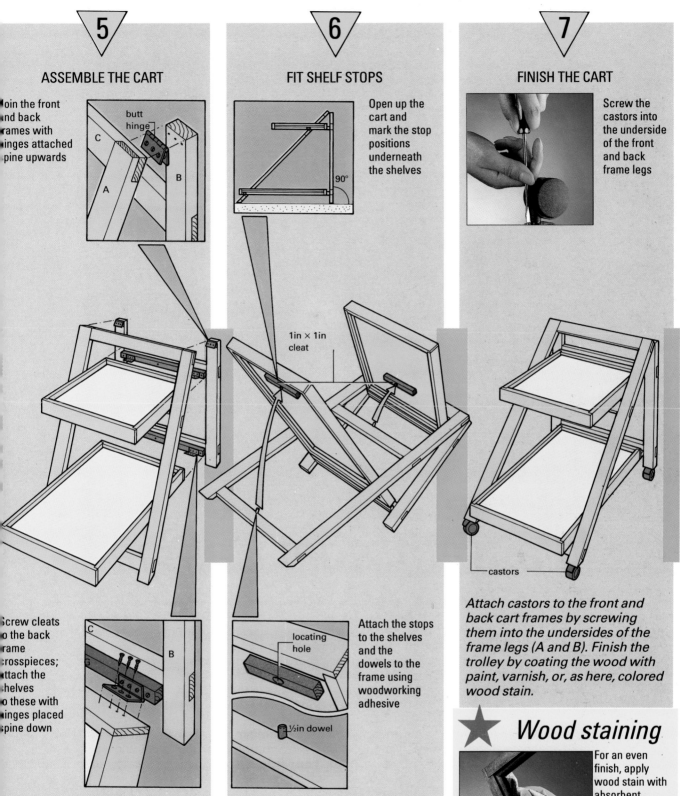

★ *Wood staining*

For an even finish, apply wood stain with absorbent paper towel or a sponge pad. Wear rubber gloves to protect your hands.

CHECKLIST

Materials
⅝in plywood
quarter-round
glass or acrylic
shaver light and socket
door hinges, handles and catches
shelf supports
dowels
¼in plywood
brads
paint
wall plugs

Tools
backsaw or saber saw
coping saw
hammer
screwdriver
tape measure and square
drill

Options
acrylic for toothbrush holder

 See Skills Guide pp. 113, 115–6, 118–9, 124, 128, 131, 138.

Build a Bathroom Cabinet

There never seems to be enough space in the bathroom for all the family's washing, shaving and toilet requisites, but this roomy cabinet is large enough for everybody's bottles, jars and potions.

Many of today's bathrooms have been built without adequate storage space, so finding room for all your toiletries can be a problem.

The bathroom cabinet has been designed with this in mind and features two roomy cupboards, each with two shelves which are easily removable for cleaning, or for storing large bottles and jars. A long open shelf runs along the bottom of the cabinet, ideal for soap dishes, toothpaste, bathroom tissues and other small items. The central mirror and shelf are illuminated by a bathroom light with shaver socket. These are available from any good electrical supplier. Make sure the one you choose is approved for bathroom use, and follow the manufacturer's instructions carefully when fitting.

Our optional toothbrush holder is made from tinted acrylic and holds three toothbrushes. You can enlarge the design to suit your own requirements.

We have used ⅝in plywood for the cabinet, with a back panel of ¼in plywood. The cabinet is assembled using dowel and housing joints, which are simple to make.

When choosing the paint for the cabinet, bear in mind that there is always a lot of condensation in the bathroom, so a polyurethane glo⟨ would be an ideal finish. Choose color to match your decor.

You can modify the cabinet to your own bathroom in several way If the cabinet is too large, it c⟨ easily be altered by removing th bottom shelf or making a one-do⟨ version. If you are thinking of redu ing the whole design, check first th sizes available in the light ar shaver sockets, as it is importa⟨ that this fits into the central se tion. Fit locks to the cupboard doo if they are to be used for sto ing medicines that may be harmf to children, and keep the key o of reach. But whatever alteratio⟨ you make, be sure to follow o basic assembly instructions on pa⟨ 138.

BATHROOM CABINET DESIGN

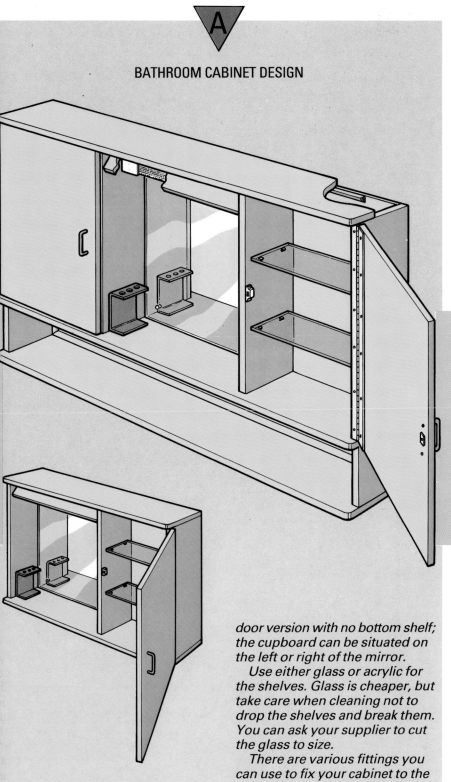

CUT THE PARTS

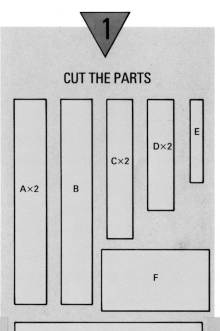

A×2 B C×2 D×2 E F G H×4

A = 7 × 43¼in
B = 6¾ × 43¼in
C = 6 × 29½in
D = 5¾ × 24in
E = 2¾ × 17¾in
F = 12¾ × 24in
G = 29½ × 42in
H = 4½ × 11⅜in

Bathrooms come in all shapes and sizes and it may well be necessary to modify the design of the bathroom cabinet to suit your needs. The alternative model shown above is a single door version with no bottom shelf; the cupboard can be situated on the left or right of the mirror.

Use either glass or acrylic for the shelves. Glass is cheaper, but take care when cleaning not to drop the shelves and break them. You can ask your supplier to cut the glass to size.

There are various fittings you can use to fix your cabinet to the wall: glass plates, which are simple fittings that screw to the top or sides of the cabinet; angle plates, triangular shaped fittings which strengthen the corners of the cabinet; and flush mount fittings, two part fittings that enable the cabinet to be removed.

Use a coping saw to round off the corners on the top center and bottom shelf. Smooth off with sandpaper

Cut parts A to F from ⅝in plywood. For the back of the cabinet, part G, use ¼in plywood. Cut the shelves, part H, from acrylic or glass. You will also need 10ft of quarter-round for the back panel.

73

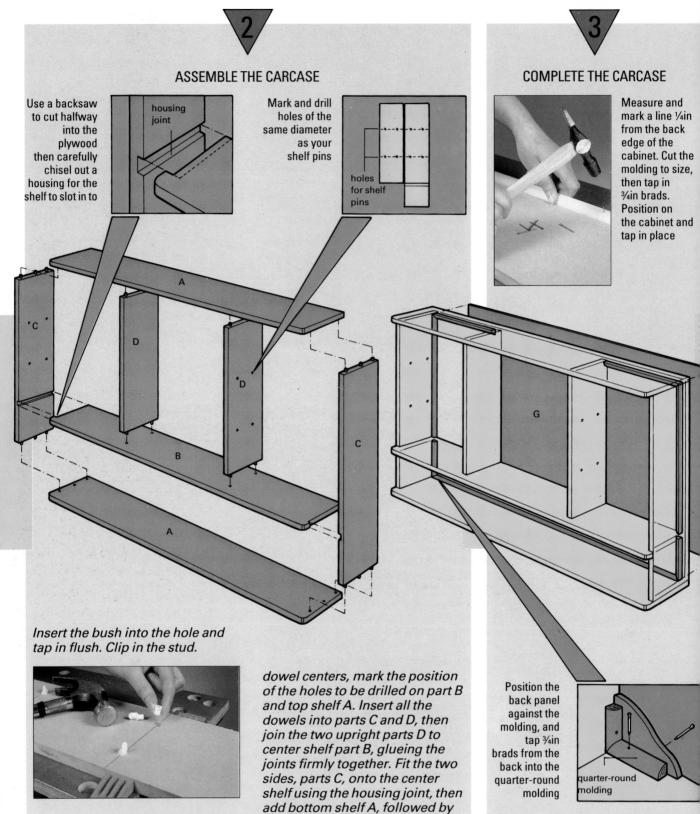

2

ASSEMBLE THE CARCASE

Use a backsaw to cut halfway into the plywood then carefully chisel out a housing for the shelf to slot in to

housing joint

Mark and drill holes of the same diameter as your shelf pins

holes for shelf pins

A

C

D

D

D

B

A

C

Insert the bush into the hole and tap in flush. Clip in the stud.

Mark out parts A and C. Drill holes for ¼in dowels using a dowelling bit. Cut the housing joints for the center shelf in parts C. Mark and drill the dowel holes and shelf support holes on parts D. Using

dowel centers, mark the position of the holes to be drilled on part B and top shelf A. Insert all the dowels into parts C and D, then join the two upright parts D to center shelf part B, glueing the joints firmly together. Fit the two sides, parts C, onto the center shelf using the housing joint, then add bottom shelf A, followed by top shelf A.

The quarter-round is used to support the inset back panel. Cut to size and fit around the inside edge of the back of the cabinet. Tack ¼in from the edge using brads.

3

COMPLETE THE CARCASE

Measure and mark a line ¼in from the back edge of the cabinet. Cut the molding to size, then tap in ¾in brads. Position on the cabinet and tap in place

G

Position the back panel against the molding, and tap ¾in brads from the back into the quarter-round molding

quarter-round molding

Once the molding has been attached, fit the back panel, part G, into the back of the cabinet, flush with the top and sides, against the molding. Using ¾in brads, tack on the back panel.

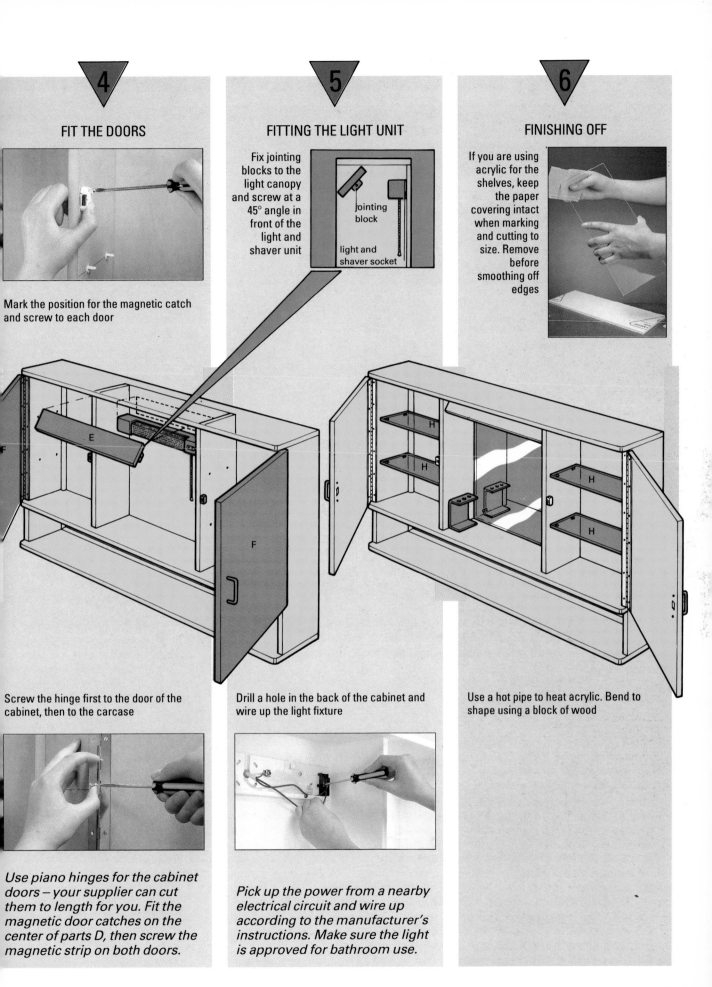

FIT THE DOORS

Mark the position for the magnetic catch and screw to each door

FITTING THE LIGHT UNIT

Fix jointing blocks to the light canopy and screw at a 45° angle in front of the light and shaver unit

jointing block

light and shaver socket

FINISHING OFF

If you are using acrylic for the shelves, keep the paper covering intact when marking and cutting to size. Remove before smoothing off edges

Screw the hinge first to the door of the cabinet, then to the carcase

Drill a hole in the back of the cabinet and wire up the light fixture

Use a hot pipe to heat acrylic. Bend to shape using a block of wood

Use piano hinges for the cabinet doors – your supplier can cut them to length for you. Fit the magnetic door catches on the center of parts D, then screw the magnetic strip on both doors.

Pick up the power from a nearby electrical circuit and wire up according to the manufacturer's instructions. Make sure the light is approved for bathroom use.

Cocktail Cabinet

This spacious cocktail cabinet is both attractive and very simple to make. The adaptable design can be altered to make display shelves, a cupboard or even a book case. Finish it with paint, lacquer or veneer to co-ordinate with the furniture in your home.

For people who like entertaining, or just relaxing over a quiet drink in the comfort of their own home, this cocktail cabinet is a must. Its simple design tones well with any decor and it provides ample room for storing bottles and decanters.

The front of the cabinet pulls down to form a handy shelf, suitable for pouring and mixing drinks. The glass shelves make an ideal display case for crystal glasses, with sliding glass doors to protect them from dirt and dust, and the two bottom drawers make a spacious store for cocktail accessories, place mats or cutlery.

The cabinet is easy to construct using plywood and simple dowel

joints. Ask your local glass supplier to cut the glass shelves and doors to size for you. They can produce the specially machined edge that you can't get if you cut the glass yourself. If you decide to use pop-in handles, ask your supplier to cut the holes for these too. However, if you decide to choose a screw-in style of handle it is easy to drill the glass at home with a glass drill bit and lubricant.

If you choose to paint the cabinet, be creative in your choice of finish. Stunning effects can be achieved using simple rag rolling or sponging techniques — paint the cabinet with a base coat, then quickly roll a crumpled rag or sponge dipped in a

complementary color over t[...] whole surface.

Make the cabinet to a size th[...] suits your room. Take into consid[...] ration the size of bottles a[...] glasses that you want to keep insi[...] and scale the cabinet accordingly.

For a cabinet of height 40in, wid[...] 5ft and depth 10in you will ne[...] two sheets of plywood. t[...] measurements of the componer[...] for a cabinet of this size are [...] follows:

A 60 × 10in
B 40 × 10in
C 29¾ × 10in
D 60 × 9¼in
E 38¾ × 10in
F 9¼ × 8⅝in
G 29¾ × 16½in
H 30 × 9¼in
I 28½ × 8⅞in
J 29¾ × 7⅞in
K 17¼ × 14⅛

COCKTAIL CABINET DESIGN

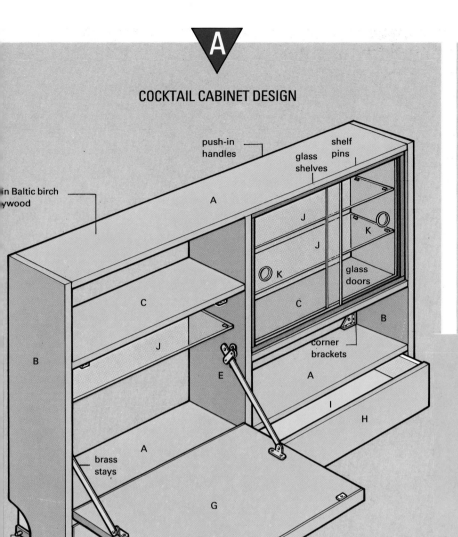

CUT THE PARTS

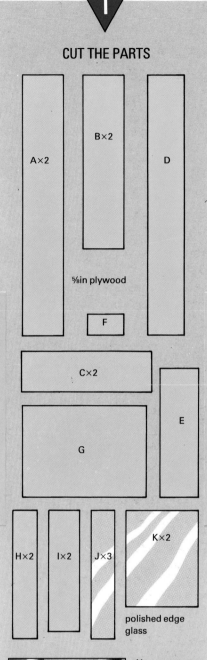

⅝in plywood

polished edge glass

You can cut the parts out with a saber saw, but a circular saw makes cutting in straight lines easier

Cut out the parts after marking and scoring the lines to avoid splintering the wood. Have the glass cut to size by the supplier, but don't order it until you've made up the cabinet.

The main carcase of the cocktail cabinet is made from ⅝in plywood. If you are going to decorate the cabinet in a finish which will show the grain of the wood – such as clear varnish – you'll need to use a quality material such as Baltic birch plywood; if you intend to paint the cabinet you can use a cheaper material such as natural pine faced plywood.

The cabinet is held square by corner blocks which also serve to attach it to the wall. You'll probably need a helper to support the cabinet while you mount it in place on the wall as it is heavy.

For mounting on a solid wall, use screws and plastic plugs; for a cavity wall it is essential to mount the cabinet directly to the framing members inside the wall skin, as the weight of the cabinet and its load combined could easily pull the attachment straight through the wallboard skin. If the framing members are not conveniently spaced you'll have to remove some of the wall's skin and insert cross-members for support.

It is best to decorate the cabinet before you mount it on the wall. Don't fit the glass until you have tested that the cabinet is securely fixed in place.

2

MAKE DOWEL JOINTS AND ASSEMBLE MAIN UNIT

Clamp the work square and use a standing try square to line up the drill

With the holes drilled, insert the dowels and assemble the cabinet dry to check for fit

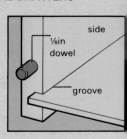

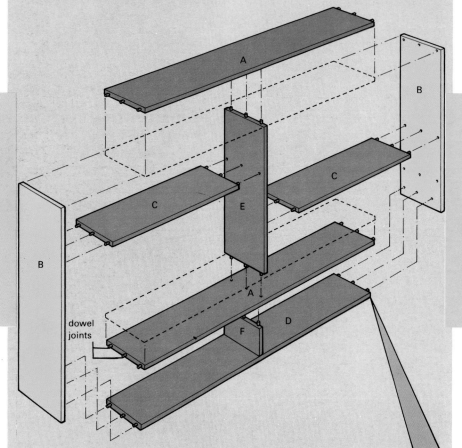

Transfer the hole positions to the other half of the joint with dowel centers one at a time or simultaneously

Stopped dowel holes are used to prevent the dowels showing on the outside of the cabinet

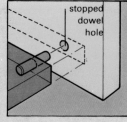

With all the parts cut out and the edges cleaned up, mark out and drill the dowel holes. Drill the holes in the edges first, then transfer the marks to the face of the other parts. Assemble the main unit on its side – don't use glue at this stage. When you're satisfied that everything fits, take the cabinet apart, reassemble it with glue and clamp it square until it is dry.

3

MAKE DRAWERS

Use dowel joints at the corners of the drawers and support the bottom in grooves cut in the front, back and sides

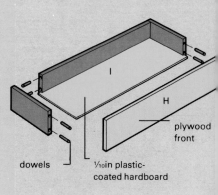

Dowel the back between the drawer sides, slide in the bottom (I), then dowel the front to the sides.

The bottom support groove in the front (H) is stopped before the ends so as not to show when the drawer is open

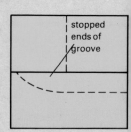

Make drawers with softwood sides and plywood front panels to fit the internal dimensions of the cabinet. The drawer runs on the bottom edge of the sides and the bottom is set in grooves.

78

4

FIX HINGED FLAP

Position the stays so they allow the flap to open until it is horizontal

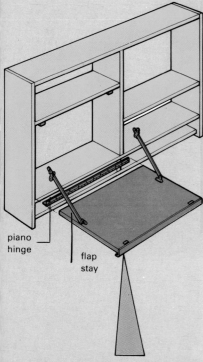

piano hinge

flap stay

Brad and glue on moldings to make the flap handle. Finish off by shaping with sandpaper

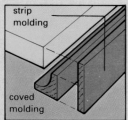

strip molding

coved molding

Add the hinging flap and its sliding stays – make up the handle before you add the flap. Don't carry out any final fixing of hardware until the paint or varnish has completely dried.

5

ADD GLASS SHELVES

The glass shelves are supported by small push-in shelf pins

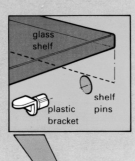

glass shelf

plastic bracket

shelf pins

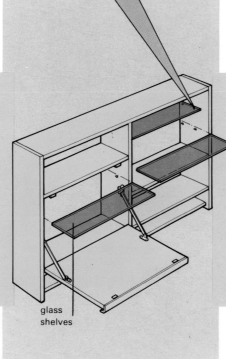

glass shelves

Mark where the shelves should go, drill holes and push in pins

Drop the glass shelves into place once you've installed their supporting brackets. The holes need to be in exactly the right place, so check your marking out several times before drilling.

6

FIT GLASS DOORS

The glass doors slide in double-channel runners fixed all around the opening

glass door

runner

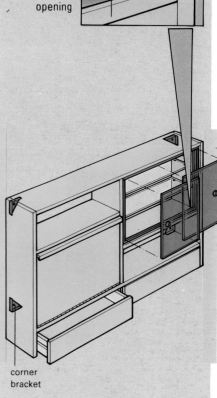

corner bracket

Tape glass for safety and insert the handles into the ready-cut holes in the doors

Screw or tack on the runners ready to take the glass doors, then add the handles. Lift the tops of the doors into the top channels and drop them into place.

Kid's Cubbyhole Bed

In small bedrooms, space for children's activities can be limited. This design rises above the problem with an exciting overhead bed with work and storage space underneath.

As children grow older and homework looms for the first time, arranging enough desk space becomes a necessity. This compact, self-contained design creates a work area and wardrobe space, as well as being an attractive and 'fun' piece of furniture in its own right. The unit is made mainly from ¾in plywood which is somewhat more expensive than chipboard, but is tougher and far smoother.

Construction is very simple — especially if you get the lumber yard to cut the sheets to size for you — although you'll find the Skills Guide, pages listed below, will come in handy.

The unit can be tailor-made to suit children of various ages and sizes — the optimum overall height for growing children is 5 feet.

CHECKLIST

Tools
saber saw/try square
electric drill and bits
screwdrivers
tack hammer/C-clamps
steel tape measure

Materials
¾in plywood
¼in plywood
1 × 2 and
1 × 1 softwood
1 × 1 softwood quarter-round
plastic joint blocks (see text)
2in diameter dowelling

See Skills Guide pp. 113, 115–6, 124–5, 134.

OVERALL DESIGN FOR AN OVERHEAD BED

The height of the bedroom unit can be varied quite easily to gain more headroom if necessary but the length and width will be determined by the size of the mattress you are using –

normally 6ft 6in by 2ft 6in, 3ft or 3ft 6in.

Height could be varied, but 5ft is ideal – it also allows ample room for desk and wardrobe suitable even for adolescents.

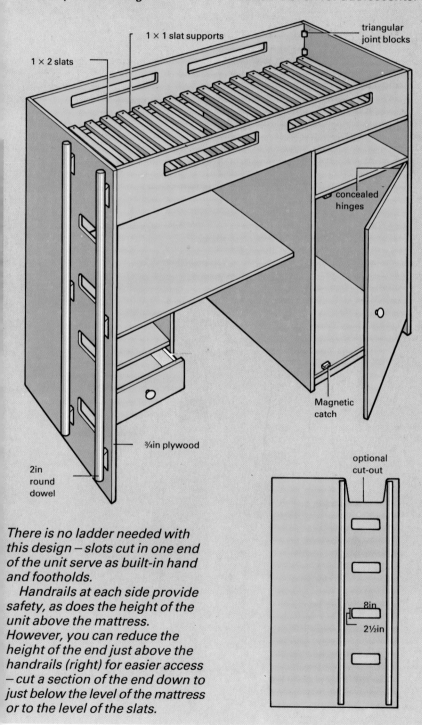

1 × 1 slat supports

triangular joint blocks

1 × 2 slats

concealed hinges

Magnetic catch

¾in plywood

2in round dowel

There is no ladder needed with this design – slots cut in one end of the unit serve as built-in hand and footholds.

Handrails at each side provide safety, as does the height of the unit above the mattress. However, you can reduce the height of the end just above the handrails (right) for easier access – cut a section of the end down to just below the level of the mattress or to the level of the slats.

optional cut-out

8in

2½in

CUT OUT WARDROBE PARTS

Start off by cutting out all the pieces you need to make the wardrobe unit. You need two parts **D** to form the upper and lower shelves. Part **C** forms the wardrobe door which is not fitted until later. You also need to cut a 47½in × 26in back panel from ¼in plywood.

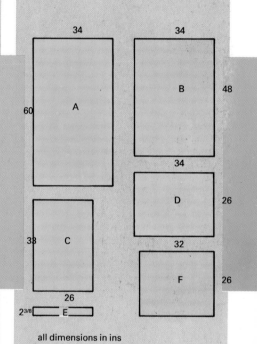

34	34
60 A	B 48
	34
	D 26
32	32
38 C	F 26
26	
2³⁄₈ E	

all dimensions in ins

Clamp a straight cleat alongside the cutting line as a guide

Adjust the blade roller guide and take great care to hold the saber saw firmly on line when you cut the board.

▽2

ASSEMBLE WARDROBE UNIT

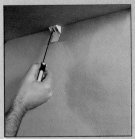

With measurements checked, drill small pilot holes and screw on the joint blocks

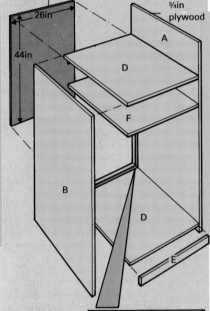

¼in plywood

26in

44in

¾in plywood

A

D

F

B

D

E

Tack quarter-round 2in in from back edge of the wardrobe. Tack the ply back panel to the molding to square and stiffen the wardrobe assembly

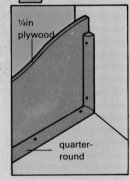

¼in plywood

quarter-round

Assemble the wardrobe – it's easiest to do this with the unit lying on its back. Notch the back corners of the middle shelf F so that it clears the quarter-round.

▽3

CUT BED AND DESK PARTS

Cut out all the pieces you need to complete the rest of the unit except the slats – cut them to length later when you've assembled the unit to make them exactly the right length.

Again, use straightedges clamped on to the work to help you cut straight lines.

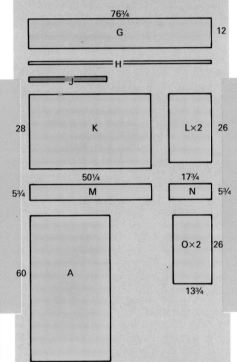

76¾

G

12

H

J

28

K

L×2

26

50¼

5¾

M

17¾

N

5¾

60

A

O×2

26

13¾

34

all dimensions in inches

Use one completed side member as a template to mark out the other

Check similar parts against each other to make sure that they match in size. Tidy up any rough or inaccurate edges with a surform plane or coarse grade sandpaper on a sanding block.

▽4

CUT THE FOOTHOLDS

Mark out the slots with a pencil. Use a template to keep to a consistent shape

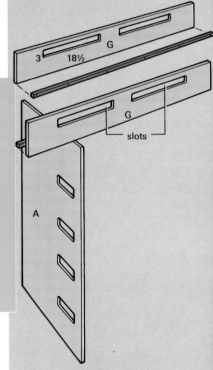

3

18½

G

G

slots

A

Cut the slots in the ladder end and side members. Positioning the hole centers depends on the size of bit used, but the edge of each hole should line up with the straight cutting lines.

Drill holes up to the inside of the corners with a large flat bit and cut between them

82

ASSEMBLE THE MAIN UNIT

Cut the slats to length. Test fit then use the first one to mark all the others

Screw attach the slats. Attach the end ones to the inside of the bed ends too

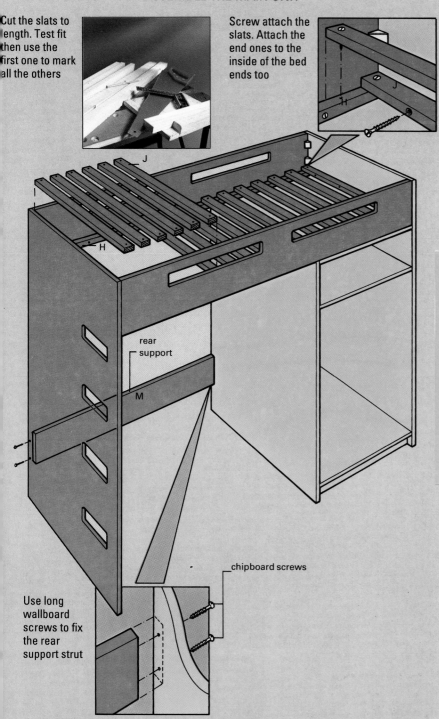

rear support

M

Use long wallboard screws to fix the rear support strut

chipboard screws

Assemble the main unit using joint blocks. Fix the ladder end to the side members first — you'll need a helper to support the assembly until it is secure to prevent splintering.

With the main unit assembled, cut the slats from 1 × 2 softwood — drill and countersink the ends. To fix them in place, stand on a chair or stool so you won't need to lean on the unit.

DRAWER ASSEMBLY

Construct 5in deep softwood drawers with side runners and the bottom supported on cleats. The false front (N) is made of plywood

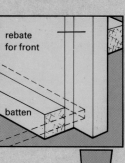

rebate for front

batten

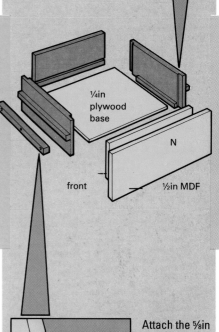

¼in plywood base

N

front   ½in MDF

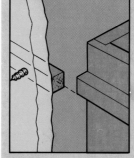

Attach the ⅝in square hardwood runners to the inside of the drawer unit with 1in screws

Make up softwood drawers with side runners (see page 13). The ¼in plywood drawer bottoms rest on ½in square cleats. Screw through the drawer fronts into the false fronts (N).

FIT DESK AND DRAWER

Measure the desk height and mark at each side to check for level

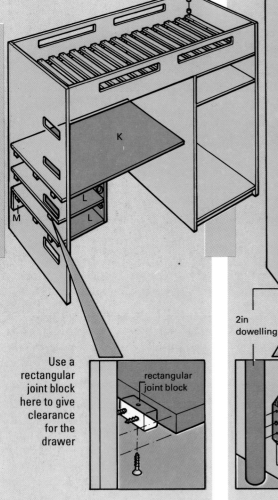

K

L

M

L

Use a rectangular joint block here to give clearance for the drawer

rectangular joint block

*Build the desk and drawer unit from parts **K, L** and **O**, and then fit it up to the main assembly. The bottom of the drawer unit screws down onto the horizontal strut at the rear.*

FIT DOOR AND HANDRAILS

Make the handrails from 2in dowelling screw-attached on each side of the ladder slots. Nail through the spacer blocks to

hold them in place until you get the screws in. Fit handles to the door and drawer and hang the door using concealed hinges. Fit a magnetic cupboard catch.

K

59½

L

N

C

¾in plywood

2in dowelling

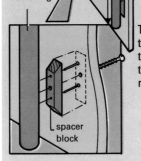

spacer block

Temporarily tack the spacers to the handrail, then screw the rails into place

Smooth down and paint the unit when it is complete, using lead-free paint. Remove handrails first

To complete the bedroom unit, make a final check on the tightness of the joint blocks, check that the drawer runs smoothly, then smooth down all rough or unfinished edges.

Paint the unit after first removing the handles, drawer and handrails to paint separately. Use a primer coat and two gloss coats for even coverage – lightly sand down after the primer/undercoat

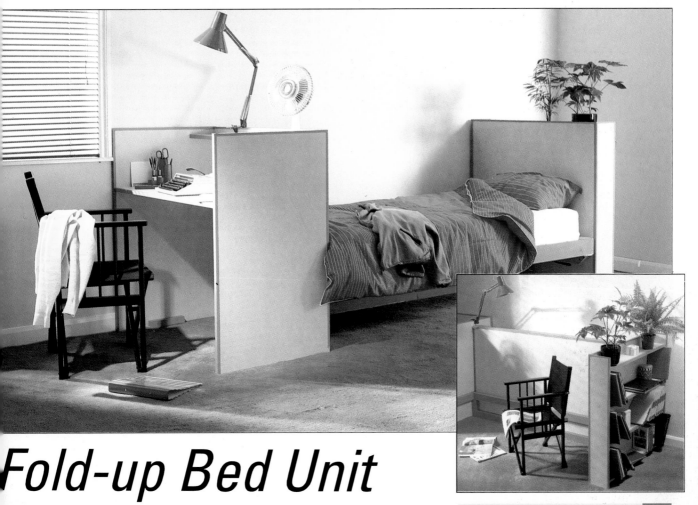

Fold-up Bed Unit

In small bedrooms, you may not have space for several items of furniture – this design gets around the problem by combining bed, desk and shelving in one unit.

All items of furniture need a certain amount of space around them so you have room to move and easy access to everything you want. The problem is that with many small items of furniture, all requiring a neighboring floor area, the available space in a small room quickly becomes used up. A solution is to combine the essential items of furniture in one unit – that way, the need for space around each item is partially eliminated. And when this bed isn't in use, you can even fold it up out of the way to release more space – either to create a roomy alcove to stretch out in, or as an area

in which to stand less important items of furniture when you want to use other parts of the room or create more formality.

Apart from the versatility of the bed itself, this design also provides a useful working space at a large desk forming one end of the bed, as well as space for books and other small items in shelves forming a complementary unit at the other.

Both the bed and the end units are easy to make – forming halving joints is the most difficult operation you'll have to do. However, the end units must be fixed to the floor to provide a secure base when the bed is being folded up – this will be easy with a wooden floor, but with concrete you'll have to drill the floor and use masonry plugs.

There are plenty of ways to amend the design too; you could add a base panel to transform the raised bed into a bench.

CHECKLIST

Tools
saber saw and straight edge
electric drill and bits
countersink bit
screwdrivers
try square/bradawl
dowel centers
marking gauge

Materials
¾in plywood (two sheets)
Softwood: 2 × 3
1 × 3, 1 × 2
½in × ¾in
4in heavy duty butt hinges
3in sliding barrel bolts
assorted screws

See Skills Guide pp. 113, 116, 118, 121, 124–5, 127–9, 132.

FOLD-UP BED WITH DESK AND SHELVES

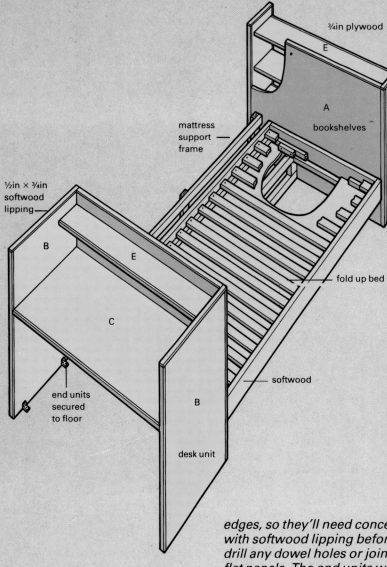

¾in plywood

E

A

bookshelves

D

mattress
support
frame

½in × ¾in
softwood
lipping

B

E

fold up bed

C

softwood

end units
secured
to floor

B

desk unit

The end units are made from sturdy ¾in thick plywood – the width is related to your mattress size. The plywood panels are held together with dowel joints and glue, which avoids exposing any ugly screw heads. It is possible to reinforce the joints with screws, but only if you will be painting the unit instead of varnishing it – the heads will need to be deeply countersunk and the holes filled afterwards.

Cut plywood has unsightly edges, so they'll need concealing with softwood lipping before you drill any dowel holes or join the flat panels. The end units will have to carry high loads when the bed is in use or being flipped up to the folded position, so it's best to anchor them to the floor with screws – use wallplugs to attach to a concrete floor.

The bed itself is simple but attractive, and is constructed from softwood (nominal sizes given). A lightweight plywood panel hides the mattress support slats when the bed is folded up. Add slats to the bed supports to transform the folded bed into a bench.

CUT END UNIT PARTS

Use the first component of each size to mark out its double before you cut it out

41in

all dimensions in inches

¾in plywood

A×2   41

23⅝   6¼

B×2   41   D×2

2¾×1¼

23¼   5½

L×2

79

M×2   10

C   41   E×5

N×2   26

Work out a cutting list – the sizes shown are for end units to suit a bed for a standard single mattress, but you can vary them as desired. If you use a saber saw to cut the parts, clamp a straight edge to the board as a cutting guide. Trim to accurate sizes specified.

ASSEMBLE AND COMPLETE THE END UNITS

Tack and glue on softwood lipping before you mark and drill any of the dowel holes

1in brads

lipping

¾in plywood

Insert all the dowels, add adhesive, assemble; clamp units square until dry

dowel holes

dowels

Drill and countersink cleats to form inexpensive joint blocks

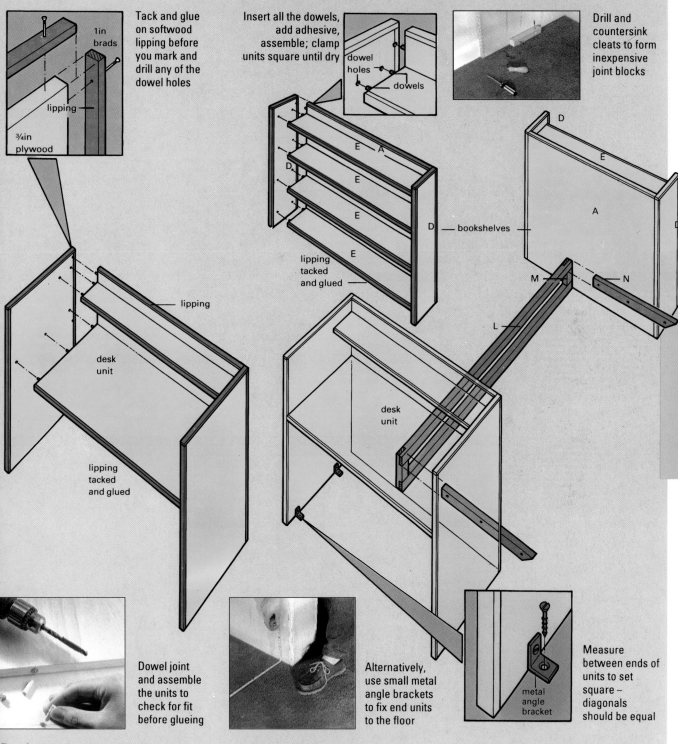

D

E

A

E

A

E

E

E

D — bookshelves

lipping tacked and glued

M

N

L

lipping

desk unit

lipping tacked and glued

desk unit

Dowel joint and assemble the units to check for fit before glueing

Alternatively, use small metal angle brackets to fix end units to the floor

metal angle bracket

Measure between ends of units to set square – diagonals should be equal

Don't start to assemble the units until you've fixed the lipping and allowed it to dry. Mark out the center lines of the panel joints and drill holes for the dowels – drill

the panel edges first, then use dowel centers to transfer marks to the corresponding panel faces. With depth-stopped holes drilled in the panel faces,

assemble and clamp the units. Join the end units by screwing to the bed support frame: finally, fix the assembly to the floor – allow for length of mattress and bed.

PREPARE THE BED PARTS

Cut the first mattress support slat and use it to mark the length of all the others

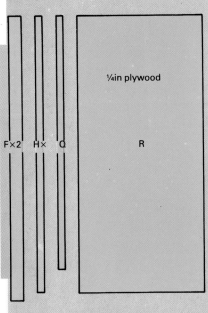

¼in plywood

F×2 H× Q R

P×3 □O×2

G×2 J×2 K×15

softwood
all dimensions
in inches

K = ⅞ × 2¾

F & G = ⅞ × 3¾

H, J, O, P & Q = ⅞ × 1¾

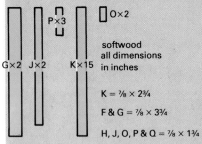

Cut out the components for the bed itself – most are softwood, so use a tenon saw and a bench hook, if possible, to avoid splintering the wood. The plywood panel for the underside of this bed measured 77in × 35¾in, so you'll have to cut it from a full-sized standard sheet using a saber saw.

MAKE BED BASE

Attach the mattress support cleats to the bed side members – allow for recessing the thin panel

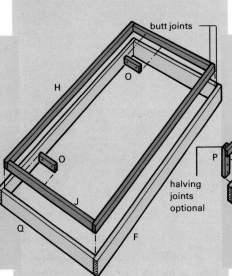

butt joints

H

O

O

J

Q

F

P

halving
joints
optional

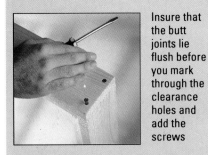

Insure that the butt joints lie flush before you mark through the clearance holes and add the screws

*Assemble the main bed frame – the corners are butt joined so allow for this when you add the cleats. Parts **O** are to give extra support for the hinges – fix 8in from the bed's back edge.*

ADD MATTRESS SUPPORTS

Attach the mattress side supports – drill and countersink clearance holes first

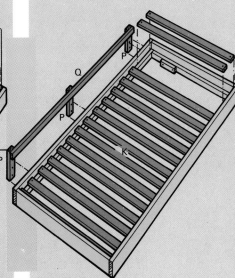

I

P

Q

P

P

K

Space out the slats which support the mattress and screw them into place

Fit the mattress side supports and the support slats next – the slats improve the rigidity of the bed considerably, but check that the frame lies absolutely flat and level as you tighten the screws.

FIT THE PLY PANEL

Reduce the size of the plywood panel slightly with a plane if it does not fit

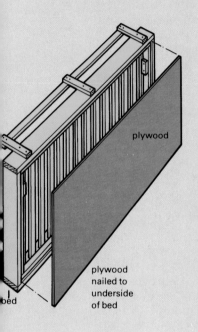

plywood

plywood nailed to underside of bed

bed

Nail the panel into place once you have trimmed it to size

Complete the bed assembly by concealing the mattress support slats with the thin plywood panel – you may have to use a plane to relieve parts of it so it fits into the recess under the frame.

FIT HINGES AND LOCKS

Heavy butt hinges hold the bed to its support frame. Attach the hinges to the cross bar first

underside of bed

butt hinge

halving joint

Attach the barrel bolts to the underside of the bed – recess them if you want a neater finish

sliding barrel bolt

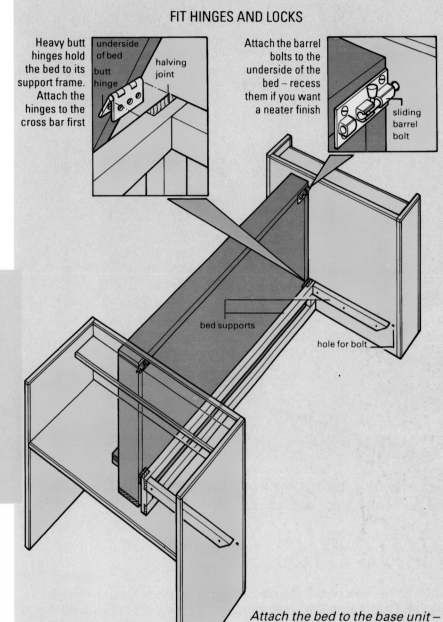

bed supports

hole for bolt

Attach the bed to the base unit – attaching the hinges is tricky, so temporarily remove the bed support frame for access if you have space problems.

If you fix the hinges to the support frame first, use a straight edge to set them flush

With bolts in place, mark where sliders hit base unit – drill ⅜in deep holes to accept them

Materials
¾in planed mahogany (1in thick
    before planing); amount
    depends on widths available
PVA adhesive
dowels and dowel centers
castors
mahogany wood stain
varnish

Tools
crosscut saw or circular saw
saber saw
pencil and string
router
half round router bit
drill
drill bits
T-bevel
miter block
protractor
screwdriver
straightedge

 See Skills Guide pp. 113,
117, 119–22, 125–6, 128,
135–6.

Bookcase on Wheels

Capture the aura of the thirties with this stylish, revolving round table and bookcase. Made in solid mahogany, it's treated with a grain enhancing stain and a deep gloss finish to give it a really traditional look, and features open sides divided into handy display shelves to house books, magazines and ornaments.

This combined bookcase and occasional table is made after a design that was very popular in the early part of this century. It is mounted on castors (which are concealed behind a plinth attached to the table's base) so it can be moved very easily and turned around even when it's heavily loaded with books. When it's not in use you can simply slide the table into an unobtrusive corner of the room.

The area below the table top is divided up into a number of different size compartments ideal for displaying books and ornaments of all shapes and sizes. There is also a tall, narrow section that's designed for more flimsy magazines or taller books which are supported by the dividing walls.

To give the table a really professionally made look, the edges of the top, base and sides are shaped

into neat bevels with a route Although using a router makes lig work of this task, you can achiev the same effect by first planing th edges then sanding them to a pe fectly smooth finish.

As it is a traditional piece of furr ture this design has been made o of solid mahogany. In its natur state new mahogany is quite a ligh pinkish colored wood, but to add th color and patina of age the woc here has been treated with mahogany stain (there are sever shades available) to match oth period furniture. The high glos finish is achieved by coating th stained wood with a brand-nam varnish. However, for an authent period feel you can apply Frenc polish (see Skills Guide p. 136).

Mahogany is a comparatively e pensive wood, but there is r reason why you shouldn't make th table from softwood such as pir and then stain it.

THE DESIGN

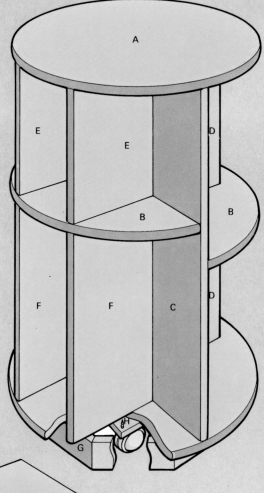

The bookcase is constructed using simple butt joints, glued and dowelled together. The skill comes in finishing off the edges to an even, rounded profile (easy if you have a router) and in varnishing the wood to a high gloss finish.

There is great scope for altering the basic design. The overall dimensions can be changed very easily – for instance you could reduce the height and make the table area wider.

Another idea is based on a design for an Edwardian bookcase. This has a central square pillar, which acts as the main support for the shelves, and upright panels on the sides to stop the books falling over.

CUT OUT THE PARTS

First assemble the separate lengths of wood to make panels of the correct width. Glue and clamp until set

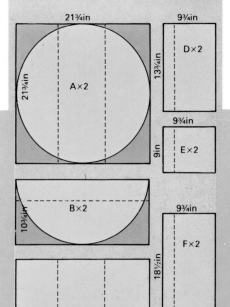

all dimensions in inches

Mark out the circles using a pencil and a length of string looped round a nail in the center

You will have to make up the panels using whatever widths are available, then cut the straight lines with a crosscut saw or power saw and cut the curved lines with a saber saw.

SHAPE THE EDGES

For the straight lines, guide the router against a straightedge clamped parallel to the edges of the wood

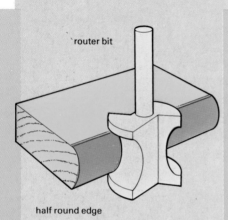

router bit

half round edge

For the curves, use a makeshift extension piece to guide the router around the circle

All the outer edges of the bookcase are shaped to a curved profile to give a professional looking finish. You can do this with a plane and sandpaper, but it's quicker using a router.

FIT THE MAIN DIVIDER

Drill dowel holes in the edges of the divider and shelves, then insert dowel centers to mark the holes on the panels

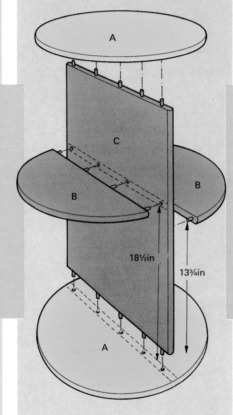

A

C

B

B

18½in

13¾in

A

Use a drill stop when drilling into the face of the panels to guard against drilling through to the other side

Mark and drill dowel holes in the main divider, the circular top and bottom and the shelves. Insert the dowels to check the fit and make adjustments as necessary, but do not glue up at this stage.

FIT THE UPRIGHTS

Mark the position of the uprights on the shelves then drill and fit dowels for each piece

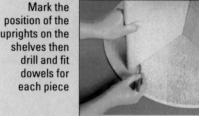

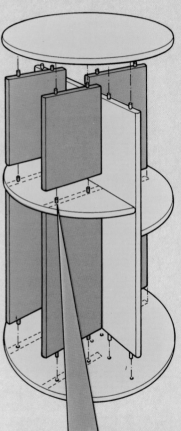

Drill holes right through the shelves and insert longer dowels to fit into the upper and lower dividers

2in long dowels

drilled right through

Work out where you want the dividers then mark their position and drill and fit the dowels. Drill right through the center shelves to make sure the top and bottom dividers are in line. Do not glue.

5 ASSEMBLE THE UNIT

Build up the unit from the bottom, glueing each section in place with woodworking adhesive

6 MAKE THE PLINTH

Cut the eight sections for the octagonal plinth, mitering the angles at 67½° as shown

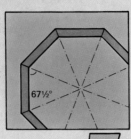

7 FINISH OFF

Fit the castors to the mounting blocks then screw the blocks to the base of the unit

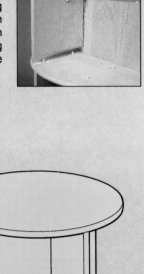

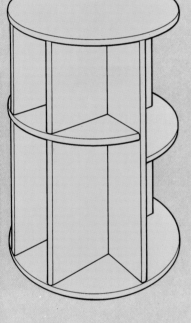

glued joints

octagonal plinth

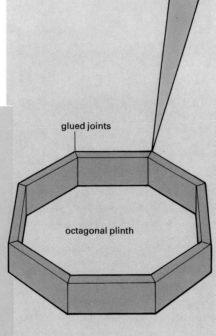

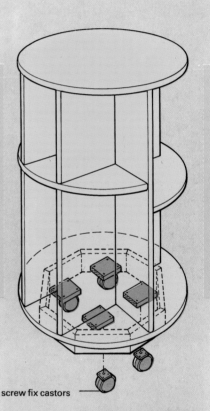

screw fix castors

Lastly, fit on the top of the bookcase, make sure everything is square and leave to dry

Glue the sections together, holding them with masking tape until dry, then glue on the base

Finish off the unit with a mahogany stain and seal with two or more coats of polyurethane

Assemble and glue the sections one at a time. Fit the main divider first, then the lower uprights and the shelves. Insert the long dowels then the upper dividers and, finally, the top.

Using a protractor, set a T-bevel to 67½° and make a saw cut at this angle in a miter block. Use this to miter the plinth sections then glue them together and glue the plinth to the base.

Measure the depth of the castors and fit mounting blocks so the wheels project below the plinth. Finish with a mahogany stain and two coats of polyurethane, sanding between coats.

Bedroom Dresser

This dual-purpose dresser combines the practical advantages of a simple vanity unit with the luxury of an elegant dressing table – and it's surprisingly simple to make.

In bedrooms where space is limited, it's often luxury items that have to be sacrificed. This practical design combining vanity unit with dressing table not only saves space, but its simple lines add elegance to any room.

The sleek exterior of the dresser conceals handy storage drawers for smaller items and a shelf for linen. Above the base, the wall-mounted shelving unit is ideal for toiletries. Matching mirror and door trims make the two parts of the dresser seem like an integral whole.

Making the dresser is simple – the base is assembled with joint blocks, and only basic butt joints are needed to make the drawers and shelves. Here, plywood-veneered chipboard is used for the main components.

If you already have a basin, adapt the dresser's design around it.

CHECKLIST

Materials
⅝in veneered plywood
softwood cleats/hardboard
casing and half-round molding
4 flush key-on hinges
24 joint blocks
screws and brads
PVA adhesive

Tools
saber saw and tenon saw
tack hammer and screwdriver
measure and square
See Skills Guide
pp. 114–5, 125, 127–8.

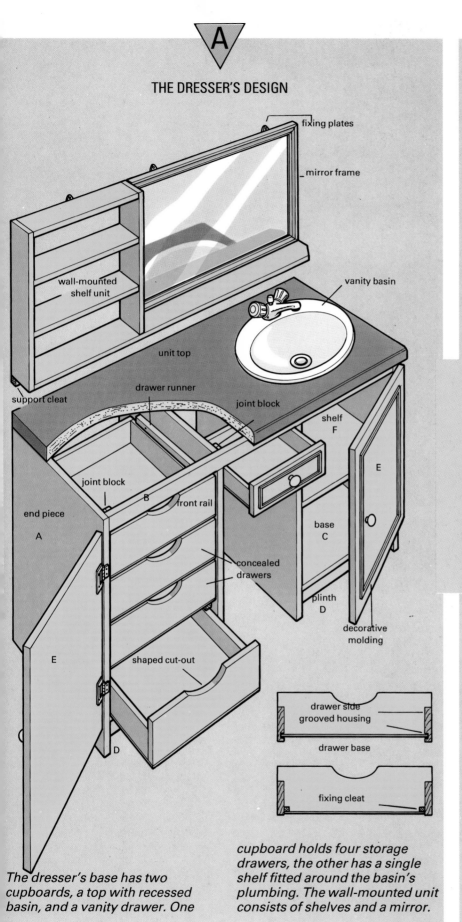

THE DRESSER'S DESIGN

fixing plates

mirror frame

wall-mounted shelf unit

vanity basin

unit top

support cleat

drawer runner

joint block

shelf F

joint block

end piece A

B

front rail

E

base C

concealed drawers

plinth D

E

decorative molding

shaped cut-out

D

drawer side
grooved housing

drawer base

fixing cleat

The dresser's base has two cupboards, a top with recessed basin, and a vanity drawer. One

cupboard holds four storage drawers, the other has a single shelf fitted around the basin's plumbing. The wall-mounted unit consists of shelves and a mirror.

CUT THE COMPONENTS

Before you cut through the veneered plywood, score along the cutting lines with a utility knife

A×4

B×2

C×2

D×4

E×2

F

Cut the components for the carcase of the base unit from ⅝in plywood. You'll need 4 end pieces (A), each 21in wide by 31½in long, 2 unit bases (C) each 21in wide by 18½in long, 2 doors (E) 19¾in wide by 26in long, 4 plinths (D) 4in high by 18½in wide and one 18½in wide shelf shaped to fit around the basin's plumbing. The front and back rails are cut from 1 × 2 softwood.

95

2 ASSEMBLE THE CARCASE

Cut 2 × 1in notches in the upper corners of 2 of the side pieces (A) for the rails

Assemble the carcase using joint blocks – you'll need a total of sixteen blocks positioned as shown

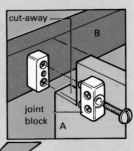

cut-away

B

joint block

A

3 MAKE THE DRAWERS

Prepare 4 18½in × 6in fronts. Cut curved finger grips on each using a saber saw

back rail

joint blocks

B

A

A

A

end piece

B

front rail

C base

D

A

end piece

C base

D

D

plinth

back

attaching cleat

base

vanity drawer

back

base

concealed drawer

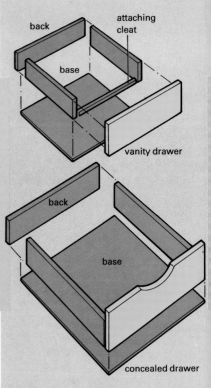

Take 2 side pieces (A) and mark off 2 × 1in notch in the upper corners of each. Cut along the marked lines using a tenon saw.

To assemble the base unit, mark fixing positions for the plinths (D) 2in in from the edges of the unit bases (C). Spread PVA adhesive along the edge of each plinth, then press it in place alongside the marked line. Secure the plinths with 1¼in finish nails

Fix 2 plinths (D) to each base (C) using PVA glue and finishing nails. Set the plinths 2in in from the base edges

spaced at about 8in intervals. Fix the joint blocks to the unit components (a dry assembly run will help you gauge their positions) then assemble all the parts of the base unit.

Make the drawers with glued and tacked butt joints. Attach sides to backs and fronts then add ⅛in hardboard bases last

Assemble the concealed drawers using 17¾in sides, 18½in backs and the vanity drawer with a 14¾in back and 11¾in side (3in wide) and a 14¾in front (4⅜in wide).

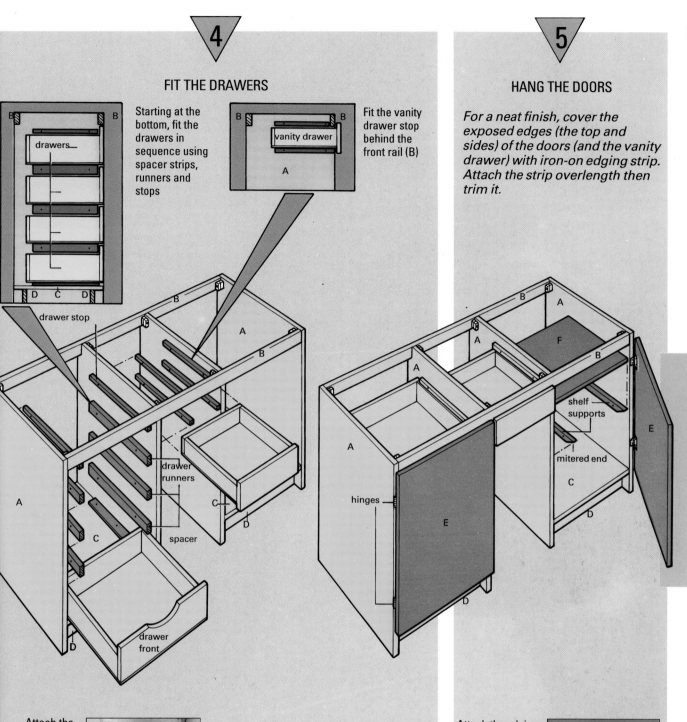

4

FIT THE DRAWERS

Starting at the bottom, fit the drawers in sequence using spacer strips, runners and stops

Fit the vanity drawer stop behind the front rail (B)

drawers

vanity drawer

drawer stop

drawer runners

drawer

C

D

spacer

A

C

D

drawer front

Attach the runners to the unit sides with 1¼in finishing nails at about 6in intervals

To fit the drawers to the base unit, you'll need a variety of runners and stops. For the

concealed drawers, first attach hardboard spacer strips to the bases (C). Mark positions for the first pair of 2 × ¾in runners. Attach the first pair with 1¼in finishing nails, then position the next two pairs in the same way. Finally, cut 2½in × ½in stops and fit them above the top drawer. For the vanity drawer, fix ¾in × ¾in runners and stops above and below.

5

HANG THE DOORS

For a neat finish, cover the exposed edges (the top and sides) of the doors (and the vanity drawer) with iron-on edging strip. Attach the strip overlength then trim it.

B

A

A

F

B

A

shelf supports

E

mitered end

C

A

hinges

D

E

D

Attach the edging by heating it with an iron. Trim it to fit in situ, using a utility knife

Finally, fit the cupboard doors. Use two hinges for each – there's no need to fit catches.

6
ADD THE TOP

Cut the top to the length of the completed unit, and to its width plus about 2in overhang. Mark basin position then cut the recess.

7
FIT SHELVES AND BASIN

The shelf unit comprises a block of 3 18½in shelves and 2 ends 18¼in and 19in high, with a 53in base shelf.

8
FIT MIRROR AND TRIM

Fix cleats to the back of the mirror frame to make a rabbet. Fix the unit with three plates

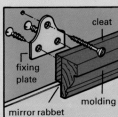

cleat

fixing plate

mirror rabbet

molding

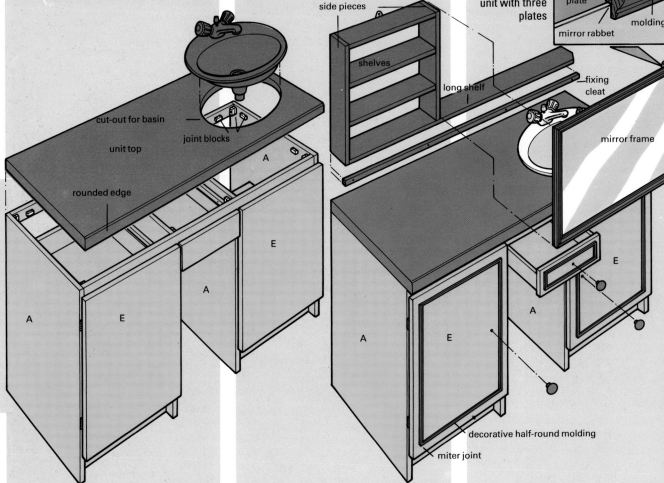

cut-out for basin

joint blocks

unit top

rounded edge

A   E

A

E

A

side pieces

shelves

long shelf

fixing cleat

mirror frame

E

A   E

A

decorative half-round molding

miter joint

Drill a starter hole inside the marked line then cut along it with a saber saw

If the top is formica covered, glue a finishing strip to the cut edges. Trim it when dry.

Fit the basin in its hole – if necessary use silicone sealant to fill the gap between the rim and the unit top

Screw a 1 × 2 cleat to the wall 6in above the top. Secure the shelf on top.

Cut lengths of ogee molding for the mirror frame and doors. Miter the ends for a neat finish

Join 2 35in and 2 18in strips of 2in molding for the mirror.

PROJECT
Writing Desk

It makes sense to centralize your 'office' by keeping all your paperwork and writing materials in one place. This writing desk has the space to satisfy those needs and is both attractive and easy to make.

If you've ever lost some paperwork or have spent time scrabbling about under a table to retrieve your last pen or pencil, you'll know how frustrating it can be not having an area set aside for writing materials and papers. If you don't have anywhere to carry out your correspondence, here's all the more reason to make a desk just for this purpose. This useful unit has all the space you'll need for storing writing materials and files in the drawer and cupboard space in the bottom half, while in the top there's room for letters, stationery and writing implements. The desk top folds out of the way when not in use, closing the desk and concealing everything inside.

Don't be daunted by the complexity of the design – the desk is made from plywood sheet, most of it of the same thickness, dowel jointed and glued together. Make the drawers as shown and use veneered plywood fronts to match the rest of the desk and to insure continuity. The unsightly edges of the plywood are covered with softwood lipping, tacked and glued in place and sanded smooth after the glue has dried. Softwood moldings are also used to make the attractive – and unique – handles for the drawers and opening flap.

The flap itself has a leather-covered writing panel. This is not inlaid – a difficult process to get right without practice – but the effect is just as good as the edges are disguised and prevented from lifting by

small-section molding, notched underneath to allow it to lie flush with the leather panel.

The door swings on flush hinges and is held shut by magnetic catches, while the opening flap is held on by a full-width piano hinge and stays shut by gravity once it is closed.

Most of the drawers slide on runners, but the large one has no runners. Instead it relies on being a tight fit in its housing in the desk so that it will be sufficiently rigid to support the writing flap when it is open.

As long as you can measure accurately and use dowels, you should have no problem in completing the unit – just check for squareness at every stage. No special tools are required either; you should find everything you need in your toolkit already.

CHECKLIST

Tools
steel tape measure
try square
saber saw
electric drill and bits
hammer
screwdrivers
backsaw
chisel

Materials
½in plywood
¼in plywood
quarter-round
softwood lipping and
  moldings
flush and piano hinges
magnetic catch for door

See Skills Guide pp. 113, 115–6, 125, 128, 133.

99

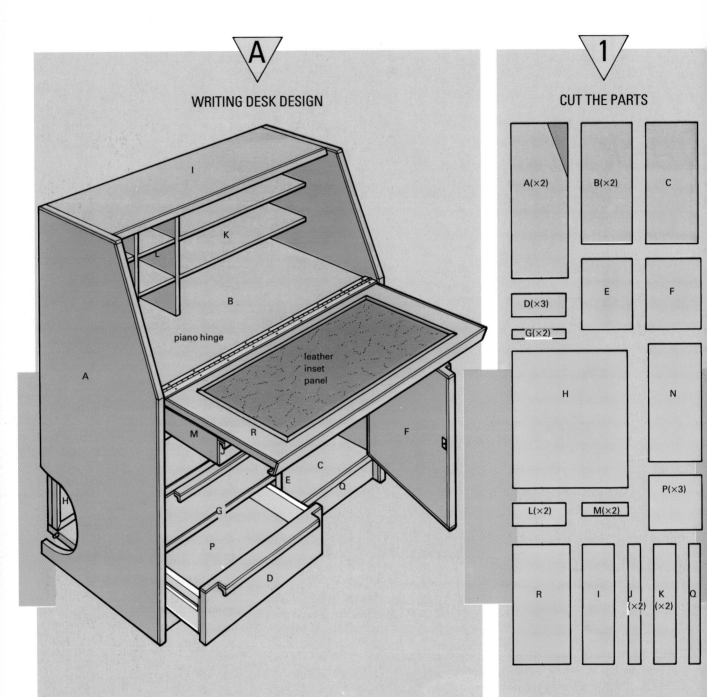

WRITING DESK DESIGN

(Labels on the exploded diagram: I, K, L, B, piano hinge, leather inset panel, A, H, M, R, F, C, E, Q, G, P, D)

CUT THE PARTS

(Parts labels: A(×2), B(×2), C, D(×3), E, F, G(×2), H, N, L(×2), M(×2), P(×3), R, I, J(×2), K(×2), Q)

The size of the writing desk can be varied – the one shown here measures approximately 46in high, 36in wide and 18in deep and will need 3 sheets of ½in plywood plus a ¼in sheet for the back panel, drawer bottoms and pigeonhole shelves. You can alter the sizes to suit your precise needs, though – for instance, the depth of the top of the desk limits the depth of the pigeonhole shelves, so you could increase this measurement if you want extra-deep pigeonholes.

You can vary the number and spacing of the shelves and dividers, and the dividers themselves can be at the left or right hand side or even right across the unit. If you don't install many dividers you'll have to tack on small-section molding to support the ends of the shelves.

If you don't feel like making all the small drawers – or if you simply don't need the space – you could always install false fronts. You'll still need the large drawer to support the flap.

Cut out the parts with a saber saw use a 1 × 2 clamped to the wood to keep the cutting line straight

Start by marking, scoring and cutting all the parts you need. Check similar parts against each other to make sure they match. Don't forget to remove the waste corners from parts A.

▽2

ADD THE LIPPING

Glue and brad the lipping in place on all the exposed plywood edges

tacked and glued

softwood lipping

A

A

A

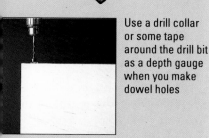

Use a drill collar or some tape around the drill bit as a depth gauge when you make dowel holes

Brad and glue on all the lipping before you mark out any of the dowel holes. Drill holes in plywood edges first, then transfer the positions to the corresponding faces with dowel centers.

▽3

ASSEMBLE MAIN UNIT

Glue and dowel the joints together. Test fit 'dry' first

glue

dowel

dowel hole

After dry-checking for fit, assemble main unit with PVA adhesive on joints and dowels

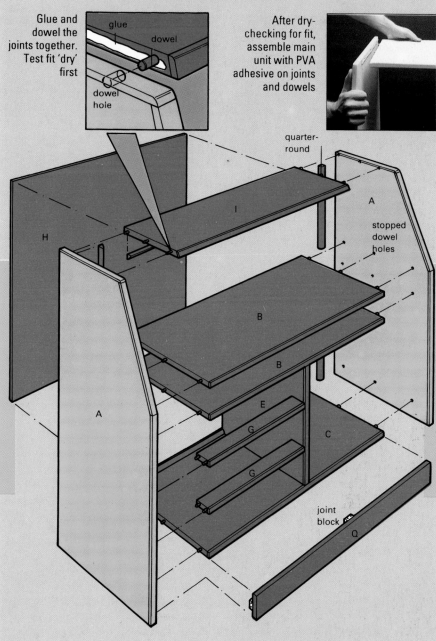

quarter-round

H

I

A

stopped dowel holes

B

B

A

E

G

C

G

joint block

Q

With the lipping glued in place and the dowels holes drilled, go on to assemble the main unit. Test-assemble the major components first to check for fit before you add glue. Fitting the

back panel will help to keep the bureau square — you need to fit the quarter-round before assembly. Part Q, with its joint blocks, will help pull the sides together during assembly.

MAKE DRAWER FRONTS

Glue moldings together to form the drawer handles. Clamp or tape them together while they are drying

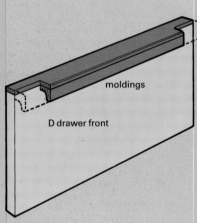

moldings

D drawer front

When the glue has dried, pin and glue the handles to the lipped drawer fronts

Make up the drawer handles from reverse quadrant molding and flat lipping. Glue and pin the handles to the lipped drawer fronts and cut away excess material. Smooth with sandpaper.

ASSEMBLE DRAWERS

Fit ⅝in square runners inside the drawer openings. They should be the thickness of part D in from the front of the unit

hardwood runner

The drawer bottoms (P) are tacked to ½in square cleats. The front is rabbeted into the sides and part D conceals the runners

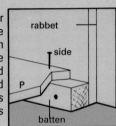

rabbet

side

P

batten

hardwood runner

P

hardwood runner

D

M

J

N

J

M

At front corners the lipping and handles cover the glued and pinned stepped housing joints neatly

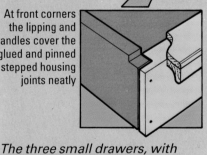

Glue together the large drawer – brads hold it until the glue dries. The bottom panel is housed into the sides and front

The three small drawers, with plywood or softwood sides, are supported on side runners of ⅝in square hardwood (see page 13). Fit the runners inside the drawer opening first and check carefully

the height of the drawer runners. The large drawer had no runners – make it to be a tight fit inside its opening as it has to support the folding flap when open.

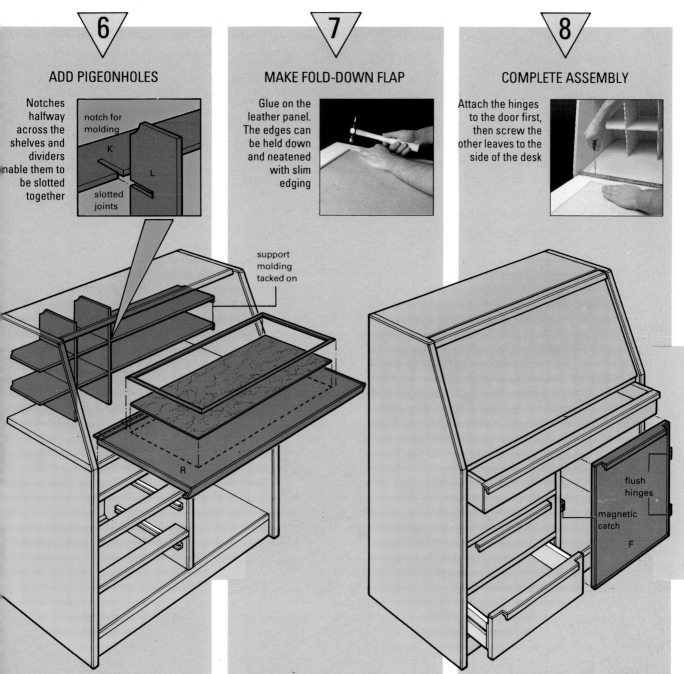

6 ADD PIGEONHOLES

Notches halfway across the shelves and dividers enable them to be slotted together

notch for molding

K

L

slotted joints

7 MAKE FOLD-DOWN FLAP

Glue on the leather panel. The edges can be held down and neatened with slim edging

8 COMPLETE ASSEMBLY

Attach the hinges to the door first, then screw the other leaves to the side of the desk

support molding tacked on

R

flush hinges

magnetic catch

F

To make the pigeonhole shelves, start by cutting strips of ¼in plywood – the width of the strip will correspond to the depth of the shelves. Cut the shelves and dividers to length – aim for a tight fit inside the desk and cut notches half-way across them so that they will slot together. Cut the notches with similar parts taped or clamped together so that the dividers will be absolutely vertical. You'll need to tack on small pieces of molding to support the ends of the shelves.

The leather panel should be glued down to prevent it from wrinkling, so spread PVA adhesive over the area of plywood to be covered and lay the leather over that. The leather panel does not have to be recessed into the folding flap as long as you cover the edges to stop them lifting. Any sort of edging or molding could be used for this, but a strip which has had its underside notched to clear the leather will sit flush with the flap surface and produce a neater job.

Lip the door and form a handle on it in the same way as for the drawer fronts, then check it for fit. Attach the hinges to the door and folding flap first, then mark their positions on the desk and screw them into place. For the sake of appearance, use very small brass screws to hold the piano hinge in place as their heads will be exposed. Finish off by staining, varnishing or painting the desk and drawers and sliding the completed drawers into place within the carcase.

Games Cart

The only space suitable for setting-up a game of chess, checkers or other board battle is usually the dining table – but mealtimes have a habit of disrupting play whether the contest is won or not. This cart has space for games, jigsaws and other trivial pursuits.

Self-confessed games fanatics will appreciate the importance of ample free space where hard-fought contests can be adjourned without having to clear up the battleground. This games cart has numerous broad playing surfaces and, as board games often use tiny, easily lost pieces, a drawer is included for storing these items.

The top of the cart is at just the right height for use when you are sitting in an easy chair, and doubles as a fold-up lid for a storage compartment. You can even run two or more games concurrently by slipping a set-up board into the tray below the top.

The cart is made from plywood with a stout softwood frame and trims. Finish it with stain, varnish or paint, clad it with laminate – or cover the playing surfaces with traditional green felt.

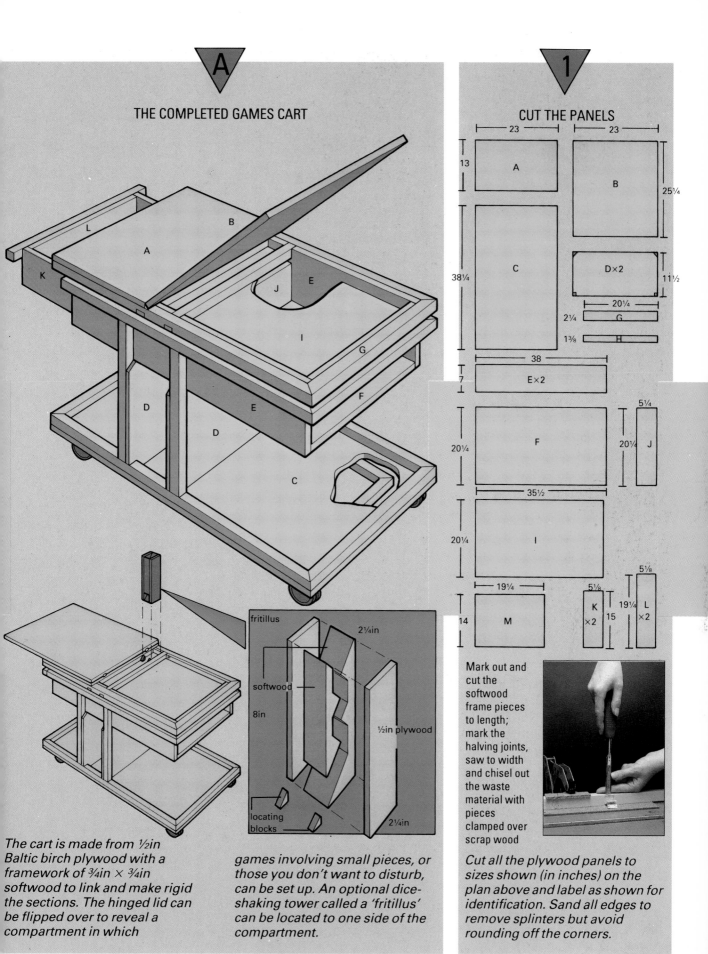

The cart is made from ½in Baltic birch plywood with a framework of ¾in × ¾in softwood to link and make rigid the sections. The hinged lid can be flipped over to reveal a compartment in which

games involving small pieces, or those you don't want to disturb, can be set up. An optional dice-shaking tower called a 'fritillus' can be located to one side of the compartment.

Mark out and cut the softwood frame pieces to length; mark the halving joints, saw to width and chisel out the waste material with pieces clamped over scrap wood

Cut all the plywood panels to sizes shown (in inches) on the plan above and label as shown for identification. Sand all edges to remove splinters but avoid rounding off the corners.

2

ASSEMBLE THE TRAY

The sides, base, central and outer dividers of the tray are assembled with PVA adhesive and brads

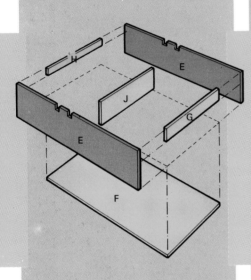

Mark out the notches, saw down the width lines then chisel out the waste

Assemble the top tray section of the cart by glueing and brading the sides to the edge of the base. Place the dividers between the side panels and secure with adhesive and brads then add the end sections.

3

ASSEMBLE THE DRAWER

Glue and brad the drawer front and back panels to the edges of the base panel then glue and brad the side panels into place. Check that the box is square

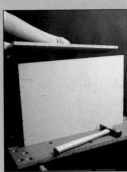

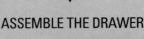

The handle of the drawer is a length of softwood, which is attached by driving brads into it through the front panel

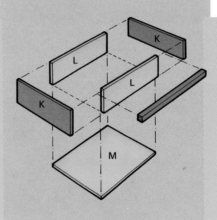

Apply adhesive to the front edge of the drawer base panel, set upright in a vice, position the front panel and brad into place. Repeat for the drawer back then apply adhesive to the exposed sides and brad on the side panels.

4

ASSEMBLE THE BASE

Brad through the underside of the base panel with the softwood trim held in a vise

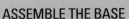

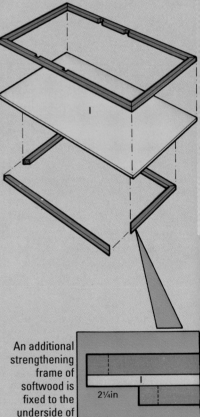

An additional strengthening frame of softwood is fixed to the underside of the base panel

2¼in

The base of the games cart is made from a panel of plywood with an edging of softwood. The softwood, mitered at the corners for neatness, has notches cut in the side lengths to accommodate the softwood uprights.

5

FIX THE UPRIGHTS

Make up two dividers from plywood panels with softwood uprights and slot the notches into the mating notches cut in the frame

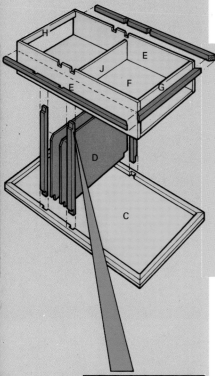

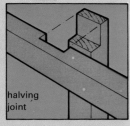

The tops of the softwood uprights are connected to the horizontal frame with halving joints

halving joint

The base of the cart is connected to the previously made tray and drawer section with two plywood dividers and four softwood uprights – the space between provides storage space for game boards.

6

FIT THE UPPER FRAMEWORK

The upper softwood frame is assembled with mitered corners and parallel cleats with halving joints

notch for softwood frame

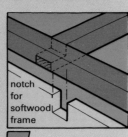

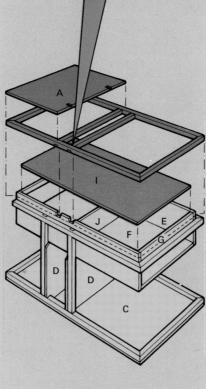

Slot in the upper frame's cross cleats. With the components clamped and glued, brad through the sides into the frame every 6in

With the tray section connected to the base via the divider panels and their attached framework, fix the compartment top panel in place. Next fit the top frame and the top of the drawer section.

7

COMPLETE THE CART

The flip-over lid which doubles as a gaming surface is attached to the fixed panel using card table hinges, the leaves of which are finished flush

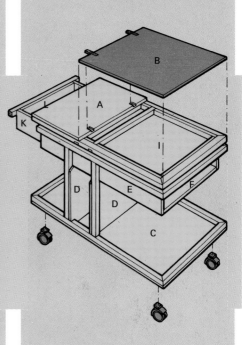

Finally, the castors are attached to the underside of the cart with screws, one at each corner

To complete the games cart hinge the flap/compartment lid to the fixed panel using card table hinges: the flap becomes another games surface at the same time revealing the compartment.

107

Curved Cabinet

This elegant display cabinet will grace any living room – its gently curved shelves are ideally complemented by a matching top and interchangeable bow-fronted storage drawers.

Here's a project that heralds a refreshing change from the harsh, angular lines of modern furniture. Curve-fronted shelves and bow-fronted drawers give it a special interest – both in its construction and in its elegant, thirties-style appeal. Ideal for displaying trinkets and ornaments, it also provides ample drawer storage space for less attractive items.

The basic cabinet carcase is easily assembled – the significant detail lies in the curved-fronted shelves which also double up as templates for the yet more attractive 'bowed' items of top, plinth and drawer fronts. These are each made from three sheets of thin plywood, glued whilst wet and formed around the pre-cut shelves – a technique with great potential.

CHECKLIST

saber saw/fine crosscut saw
drill and bits
dowel centers/adhesive
marking tools
plane or surform tool
bar clamps and C-clamps
hammer/nailset/filler
⅜in fluted dowels (1 pack)
1 full sheet of ¾in plywood
1 full sheet of ¼in plywood
½ sheet of ½in plywood
offcuts of 2 × 3 softwood

See Skills Guide pp. 113, 116, 118, 120, 125, 128.

THE CABINET'S DESIGN

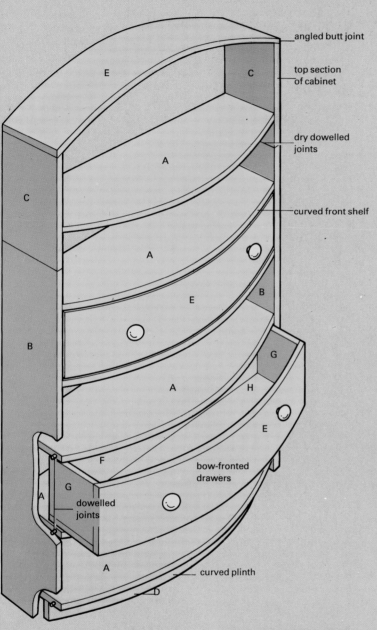

angled butt joint

top section
of cabinet

dry dowelled
joints

curved front shelf

bow-fronted
drawers

dowelled
joints

curved plinth

The basic carcase comprises two sides (B), 5 shelves (A) and a removable top section made from two side extensions (C) and a further shelf (A) – they're all made from ¾in plywood. The shelves are cut to have curved front edges and the joints between shelves and sides – and between B and C – are all dowel-jointed (see p. 128). The curved top

and bowed drawer fronts are each made from three sheets of ¼in plywood, shaped to match the shelves by glueing and clamping them to the pre-cut shelf fronts (page 110). Use a full board width for all curved components (and the plinth D), then shape to length. Use a half sheet of ½in plywood for the drawer parts; bases (H), sides (G), back (F).

CUT THE COMPONENTS

If your supplier won't cut the ¾in plywood, use a saber saw to do so yourself. Then cut the curved shelf fronts – use one as a template

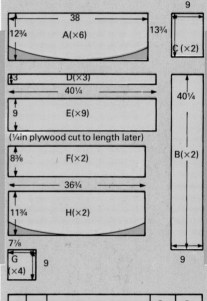

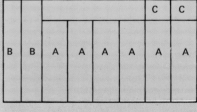

Cut the main carcase components (A, B and C) from ¾in plywood, following the dimensions and guidelines above. You'll need a full sheet of ¾in ply – use the cutting plan above. Then carefully cut the ¼in plywood for the bow-fronted drawers and the curved top (E) and plinth (D). Cut the thin ply overlength for accurate trimming later.

2 PREPARE CURVED SECTIONS

Cut all parts E overlength from ¼in plywood, then lightly spray three at a time with water to soften them. Clamp around shelf fronts and leave 4 hours. Unclamp, allow boards to dry

3 FORM THE CURVED SECTIONS

Place 3 shelves (A) on top of one another, with offcuts between. Lightly clamp, tap edges to align the three shelves, check then fully tighten

4 MAKE THE TOP SECTION

Use the bowed top to mark the angle on to C, then cut C. Nail and glue the top in place, then trim the overlength ends to match the line of C

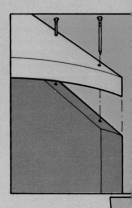

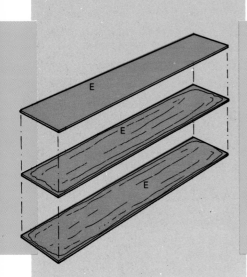

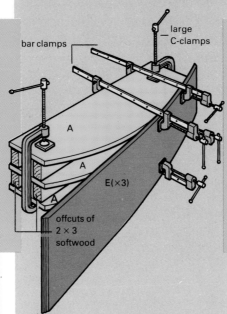

bar clamps

large C-clamps

A

A

E(×3)

A

offcuts of 2 × 3 softwood

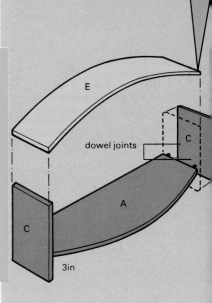

E

dowel joints

C

C

A

3in

Spread liberal amounts of PVA wood adhesive over one side of each. Press together and align the edges

Drawer fronts and top (E) and the plinth (D) are each made from three strips of ¼in plywood made moist for shaping.

Use bar clamps to bend E to fit against the shelf edge former. Keep the sheets aligned. Mark shelf edges on the inside

Use the curved shelves as a former. Use bar clamps and large C-clamps to bend the wet ply strips up to the curve.

Measure 11¾in up the edges of C, hold the top in place and mark the angle you need to cut. Square lines and cut (and plane) to shape

Make the top section from one shelf dowel-jointed to two extensions (C), with bowed top (E) nailed and glued on.

5

ASSEMBLE THE MAIN CARCASE

Square lines across B at the positions shown. Use dowel centers to mark dowel positions from A on to B. Dry assemble before glueing

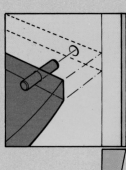

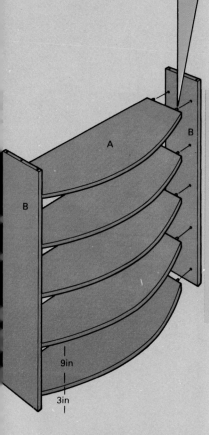

A

B

B

9in

3in

A dowel jig and dowel centers will help to make all the joints needed. Use ³⁄₈in fluted dowels, centered in the shelf edges

*Make sure all the shelves are identical; mark **B** as shown. Drill for two dowels on each shelf, use centers to mark **B**, then assemble.*

6

ADD PLINTH AND TOP SECTION

Dowel-joint C on to B, using three dowels per side. Adjust length of C and B to maintain the shelf spacings of 9in. Don't glue this joint

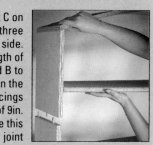

removable top section

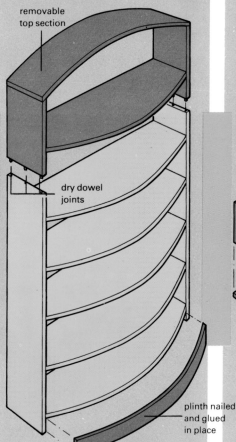

dry dowel joints

plinth nailed and glued in place

Make the plinth in the same way as the other bowed items. Trim to fit and nail and glue in position as shown

Complete the basic carcase by adding the plinth and the top section. Sand smooth and fill edges with fine filler.

7

COMPLETE THE DRAWERS

With the drawer base cut to size nail and glue the base, sides and back together. Use the base shape to trim the sides ready for the bowed fronts

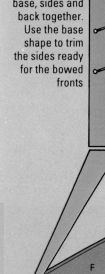

trimmed first

G

F

G

trimmed to fit

H

nailed, glued and filled

Sides and back are shallower than the drawer front – the base is nailed under them and the fronts are nailed on to base and sides

Make the drawers from ¹⁄₂in ply. Cut the base first, allowing for the thickness of the front. Assemble, then nail, glue and fill.

SKILLS GUIDE

This Skills Guide provides you with information needed to make the Indoor Projects. If you have difficulty in finding some of the materials used in your local area, there are mail order firms which sell specialist hardware, for example, European hinges, who should be able to help. Their names can be found in do-it-yourself, woodworking and cabinet-making magazines. Another source for specialist materials might be your local millwork shop or a large cabinet-making firm. Try the *Yellow Pages* too. If all else fails get advice from your local lumber yard or from an experienced woodworker for a suitable substitute.

Another point: When making projects that require carpentry, check your cutting list first, in case of difference in dimensions between your materials and those suggested here. Always take actual dimensions from the materials themselves to insure accuracy.

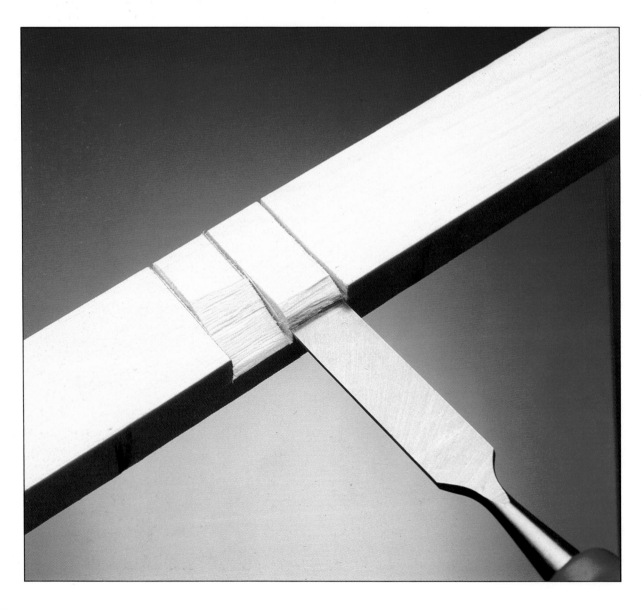

Working out cutting lists

Simple carcases

Whatever you're making, you need a detailed cutting list so you can work out the most economical way of buying materials. This applies especially to man-made boards.

Start with a simple sketch (below), containing enough detail to show how the unit is assembled – how butt joints are arranged, for example. Then write on it the overall dimensions of the unit, plus any other dimensions that depend on the unit's design such as shelf spacings and plinth heights. Label each component (use the same letter for identical components).

Next, measure the thickness of the board you're using. Now you can draw up simple plans (below right) and mark on them the actual dimensions of each component, taking into account the board thickness. Exaggerate this on the sketch for clarity.

Finally, write out your detailed cutting list (right), noting how many of each component to cut.

Rough sketch

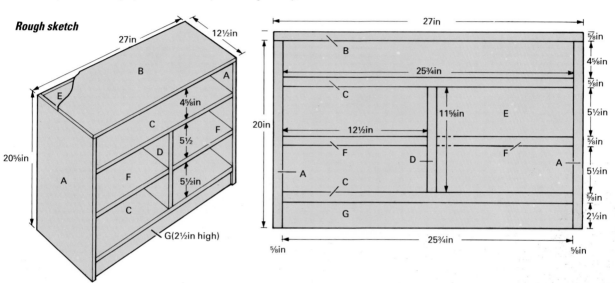

Estimating materials

Once you have a detailed cutting list, the next job is to work out the most economical way of buying your materials so as to minimize potentially expensive waste.

You must first decide on what raw material you intend to use – natural wood, raw man-made board such as chipboard, plywood or a finished board such as veneered or plastic-coated chipboard. Next you need to know the standard sizes in which it is available. There is a huge range of standard sizes for natural wood, but raw man-made boards are generally available only in 8 × 4ft sheets. You can often have sheets cut to size at a lumber yard.

With boards, work out the most economical cutting plan on paper, by drawing the components out to scale and shuffling them around on a scale drawing of the full board until you find the best fit. Cross-check by adding up component sizes in each direction.

With solid wood, simply total the lengths needed for each cross-sectional size the cutting list requires.

Specimen cutting plan

The sketches show how the components of the cutting list overleaf can be economically cut from two standard planks of finished chipboard. Each of the components is lettered to correspond with the cutting list, and waste is shaded in color.

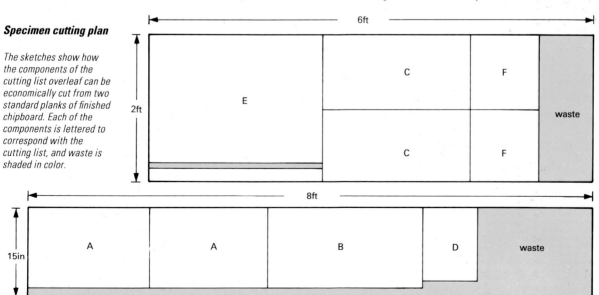

Working with coated chipboard

Cutting boards to length

Laminated chipboard is sold in full 8 × 4ft sheets in a variety of thicknesses. You can have sheets cut to size at a lumber yard or, if you own a circular saw or a saber saw, you can save money by buying a full sheet to cut down.

Whether using a power saw or hand saw, you'll need a pencil, *try square*, *tape measure*, *metal straightedge* (such as a metal ruler), *trimming knife* and something to support the board. A portable workbench is ideal for narrow boards. Wider boards are more difficult to maneuver and cut (figure 6).

When cutting *laminated chipboard* – just tape over your cutting line with masking tape. Then cut.

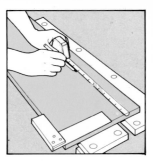
1. *Check the board end is square, then mark on the length at a number of points*

2. *Use your try square to mark across, then down the edges. Extend the square as shown*

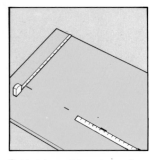
3. *Mark large sheets at a number of points and join the marks with a long straightedge*

4. *Score wood veneer on both sides to prevent splintering and to guide your saw blade*

5. *Clamp narrow boards steady as you cut and saw to the waste side of the scored line*

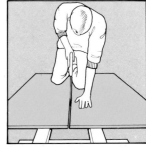
6. *If sawing large sheets, use lengths of wood to support both sides of the cutting line*

Checking measurements

Check the accuracy of all the sawn edges – they should align with your marks and be square to the surface for the entire length of the cut. Use your try square or a known straightedge to test the accuracy; use the try square to check all corners too. Save time by using one component to check the size of all matching components. Adjust large errors by re-cutting, adjust small errors by planing.

Finishing the edges

You'll need enough *matching iron-on or self-stick edging* to finish all the exposed edges of the chipboard (hidden or jointed edges don't matter) and an iron to apply it – don't use a steam iron. Trim the corners using a brand-name laminate *trimming tool* or medium sandpaper wrapped around a sanding block.

Cut-outs can be made using several saw cuts followed by a sharp chisel but will be neater if you use a coping saw. Always score along cutting lines first. Use only a coping saw for cut-outs in *laminated chipboard*.

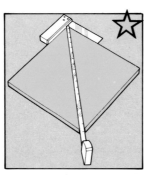
1. *Check all measurements for accuracy. Compare diagonals to check large sheets*

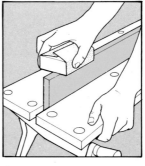
2. *Adjust small errors and smooth rough edges using sandpaper on a sanding block*

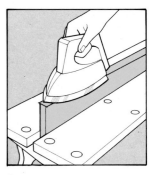
3. *Carefully iron on matching veneer along all the exposed edges using a dry iron*

4. *Trim the corners using a brand-name tool or medium sandpaper on a sanding block*

5. *Make cut-outs with a series of close saw cuts followed by trimming with a sharp chisel*

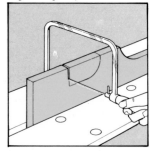
6. *Use a coping saw for a neater cut out (score all cutting lines through wood veneers first)*

Using joint blocks

One-part joint blocks

These blocks (often called modesty blocks) are used to butt-join two pieces of wood or board. They're particularly useful for assembling units made from chipboard or plywood – materials that can't readily be joined with carpentry. They're easy to use for assembly, but will not accept repeated dismantling.

The plastic or wooden blocks fit in the right-angle between abutting pieces and are fixed with screws. The basic block is a rectangle with two pre-bored countersunk holes in one side and one centrally in an adjacent side. Hollow triangular blocks have two holes in the short sides and a snap-on cover.

Screw length is an important consideration, depending on the materials you're joining: use a screw that protrudes through the block by about ⅜in – pre-packed blocks usually come with sufficient screws.

For narrow shelves, two blocks at each end are adequate; otherwise space them about 18in apart to prevent warping.

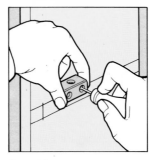
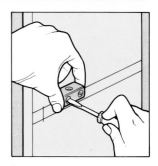

1. *Measure from the edge of the board for the adjoining panel; square parallel lines across*

2. *Place a joint block against the inner line, then start off the screw holes with a bradawl*

3. *Insert the screws and drive them in with a screwdriver. Fit other blocks in the same way*

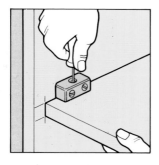
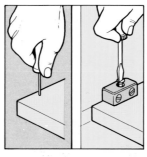

4. *Align the adjoining panel against the first, butted to the blocks. Mark through the holes*

5. *Remove the panel, start off the screw hole, return it and secure with the single screw*

6. *Fit a triangular block in the same way, using two screws per side, then snap on the cover*

Two part fittings

Two part knock-down (KD) fittings are joint blocks that can be repeatedly dismantled but which make the assembly of furniture quick and easy.

Various types are made, but most work on the same principles: the two halves of the plastic device are screwed to the components you want to join. The two halves are then held together by a machine screw and retaining bolt. Mating shapes insure accurate alignment.

Some types resemble one-part blocks – one half slots inside the other and is held by a screw-operated cam.

To attach the device, attach one half –the inner one or one with the nut, where applicable – to one panel, then join the two halves with the bolt. Align the panels to mark through the screw holes of the second half. Release the halves, attach the second half to the second panel, then bolt both together again.

Use No. 6 flathead screws, which protrude through the device by ⅜in – ideal for ½ to ¾ in boards.

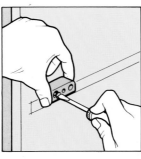
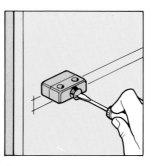
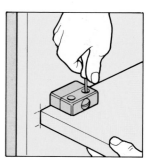

1. *Mark the position for the block on one panel, then attach the half with the nut*

2. *Attach the second half of the block to the first by tightening up its machine screw*

3. *Hold the adjoining panel in place against the first and mark through the holes*

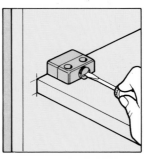
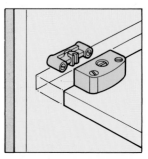

4. *Release the two halves of the block and screw the half with the bolt to the second panel*

5. *Reassemble the two halves of the joint block, tightening the screw into the nut.*

6. *With a cam fitting, fit the inner, then the outer half. Secure with a turn of the screw*

Working with plywood

Plywood is a man-made board, indispensable for constructing box furniture, shelves and other projects requiring a tough, flat surface.

Plywood make-up

Plywood comprises thin wood veneers glued together in layers. The grain of individual leaves is at right-angles to that on each side so warping is minimized. There are always an odd number of veneers – three-ply and five-ply, for instance – so that the facings run parallel.

Some plys have a decorative facing of plastic laminate, factory-applied paint or wood veneer; others have grooves to resemble panelling. Birch-faced ply is most common. Inner and outer plys should be the same wood and thickness.

Grading refers to knots, joins and defects in the facings. Double grading refers to each facing respectively. Boards are also graded by the adhesive used to bond the veneers. It is a good idea to ask your lumber dealer which grade of plywood is best for your project.

Plywood comes in standard sheets, commonly 8ft × 4ft, although smaller panels may be found. Thicknesses vary from ⅛in to ¾in.

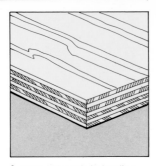

1. *Plywood is made by bonding together individual veneers of wood to make a tough board*

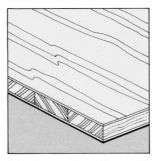

2. *Lumber core plywood has a solid core of softwood slats glued side by side with thin facings*

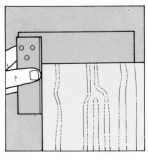

3. *Before marking out, check that the edges are at right-angles using a try square*

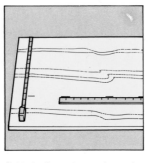

4. *Mark a large sheet at intervals and join the marks with a long straightedge*

5. *Score twin cutting lines with a knife to cope with the width of the saw blade*

6. *If sawing by hand, support the board each side of the cutting line with boards*

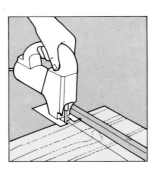

7. *Using a saber saw or circular saw is easier. Fit a fence to insure a straight line*

Edging details

With plywood the edges can be difficult to work to a neat finish.

Use solid lipping to finish the edges neatly, mitering the corners. Plain or decorative profiles can be made with a router. Simple butt-joints can be made using a single edging molding.

1. *Smooth down the rough edges of plywood using a surform tool*

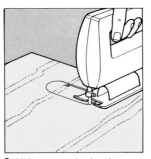

8. *Make cut-outs in ply using a saber saw. Drill a starter hole for the saber saw blade.*

2. *Fit hardwood lipping with PVA glue and brads driven in dovetail fashion*

3. *Use lipping to butt-join panels. Sand the edging flush with the board surface*

Choosing hardwoods

Hardwoods are used for their natural beauty – attractive colors, complex grain patterns and fine textures – and are mainly reserved for furniture-making. Generally speaking, they are considerably harder than softwoods but there are exceptions; for example, balsa is termed a hardwood in spite of the fact that it is extremely soft and light.

Hardwoods shouldn't be painted, but rather varnished, waxed, oiled or polished to enhance their appearance – different woods need different treatment.

Standard sizes aren't available. To buy hardwood you must calculate the total volume of wood needed in board feet for each thickness used. Get advice from the lumber yard on what waste factor to add on.

Hardwoods are sometimes used as thin veneers over man-made boards to produce the look of solid wood at less cost. Veneers are pressed and glued over the boards and this makes them vulnerable to damp when they start to blister and bubble.

Softwoods come in a range of standard lengths, widths and thicknesses. The planed size (actual) is less than the sawn (nominal) size. Again, get advice from your lumber yard on the choice of softwood for your project.

Choosing softwoods

Softwoods are cut from coniferous (cone-bearing) trees such as spruce, pine, larch and fir. The classification 'softwood' is botanical and many types are dense. Choose softwoods for floorboards, joists, rafters and for some joinery – door and window frames are commonly made of softwood.

In their favor softwoods are easy to saw, chisel, plane and sand; they hold screws well, too. But, although they are strong along the grain, they're weak across it, and nails can cause splitting which not only looks ugly but also reduces the strength of the fixing. You can avoid splitting timber by using finishing nails.

Softwood is porous, so can't be used outdoors without the protection of paint, varnish or preservative. It's sold planed on both faces and edges. Nominal sizes will differ from actual sizes.

1. Sight along planks to check for warps and twists due to uneven drying during seasoning

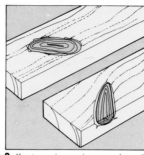

2. Knots oozing resin are awkward to cut and finish; dry loose ones may even fall out

3. End shakes are splits along the grain; cup shakes are splits along the annular rings

Hardwoods and their Properties

type of hardwood	properties				
	shade (1=palest 3=darkest)	lustre (1=lightest 3=deepest)	grain (1=straightest 3=most variable)	durability (1=least durable 3=most durable)	density (1=most dense 3=least dense)
Afrormosia	3	3	3	1	1
Ash	2	2	1	3	1
Beech	2	3	2	3	2
Elm	2	2	2	3	1
Mahogany	3	3	1	1	3
Oak	1	2	2	1	1
Sycamore	2	2	1	1	2
Teak	1	1	1	1	1
Walnut	2	3	2	3	1

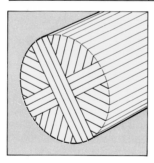

1. Tree trunks may be cut by quarter sawing to yield similar graining throughout

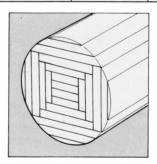

2. Tangential sawing gives wide planks from fairly small logs with a plainish, open grain

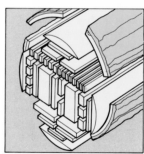

3. This gives thin boards outside; thick planks inside; and waste wood for pulp

Measuring and marking wood

Marking to length

Once you've established a squared end of your workpiece you can accurately mark the piece to length.

To do this you'll need a steel tape measure (for long or short lengths) or a boxwood or plastic folding rule for precision on shorter lengths. Measure the length you want from the squared end and draw a 'V' in pencil.

Hold a try square tight against the wood and scribe across with a sharp trimming knife at the marked point.

Repeat marking

Mark out several pieces of wood to the same length at once.

Select face sides and edges then tape the pieces together with one set of ends aligned squarely.

Lay the wood on a flat surface then square off the taped-together ends using a try square and marking knife. Measure the length required from the outer pieces and square off with the try square from both sides. Scribe around and cut the individual pieces in the normal way.

Marking a square end

Accurate measuring and marking is vital when cutting timber to length: errors tend to multiply and could result in sloppy joints and crooked construction.

Select the piece of wood you want to cut to length. Hold a try square on adjacent sides and edges to determine which are the most accurate right-angles: slide it along the wood and check by looking for gaps under the blade.

Mark the truest angles with pencil symbols 'f' and 'V' (see 2) to indicate face side and face edge respectively. Always work from these marks to insure consistent marking out.

Before you cut a piece of timber to length, first insure that it has one perfectly square end from which you can take the second measurement. Hold the try square on the face side, about 2in from the end, and scribe a line across with a sharp trimming knife. Turn the wood to the face edge and continue the line, then take it onto the remaining edge. Join the two edges on the final side. If the wood is square, the lines should meet.

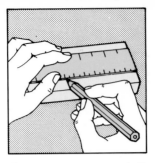

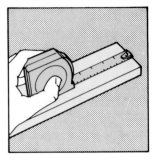

1. *Measure from the squared off end with a steel or folding rule and mark the cutting line*

2. *Square around the wood with the knife held against a try square*

3. *On a very long piece of wood it's best to use a steel tape measure*

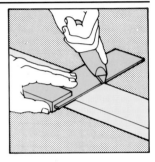

1. *To cut several pieces to the same length, tape them together and square off the ends*

2. *Measure and mark the length of the pieces from both sides of the bundle and square off*

3. *Release the separate pieces, then scribe around each one with a try square and knife*

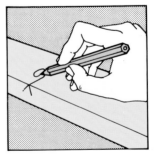

1. *Use a try square to find out which two sides of the wood are perfect right angles*

2. *Mark the face side and face edge in pencil with an 'f' and a 'V' respectively*

3. *Square across the face side of the timber using a try square and a sharp trimming knife*

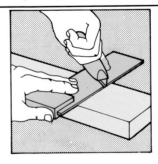

4. *Turn the wood to the face edge and continue the score line across with the knife*

5. *Flip the wood onto the other edge and scribe the line; turn it onto the final side*

6. *Cross-hatch the waste area beyond the scribed line to indicate the part to be cut off*

Marking curves and angles

Marking curves

Most of the curves cut in carpentry are circles or sections of circles, and so can be marked out with a compass either bought or improvised.

For circles up to about 6in across, an ordinary drawing compass is ideal. The best type has an interchangeable point and pencil so it can be used as dividers; you get a more accurate mark using the latter since the sharp point scores the wood surface more accurately than a pencil. Dividers are useful for other marking-out jobs too, like dividing planks into sections of equal width.

For larger circles a home-made beam compass is the best answer. Cut a length of scrap wood to roughly the radius you want to draw out. Then drive a nail through one end to act as the pivot, and another at the other end to scribe the circle. Drill a hole for a pencil if you prefer.

To mark out very large circles use a length of wire – string may stretch.

For irregular curves, use a template or an artist's French curve.

1. Use a drawing compass or dividers to mark out circles up to around 6in in diameter

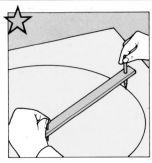

2. For larger circles, improvise a beam compass with a wood offcut, a nail and a pencil

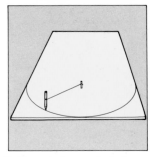

3. Alternatively, use wire to draw out large circles – it's less likely to stretch than string

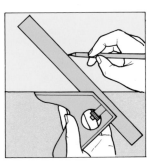

4. For some curves, it may be more convenient simply to draw round a household object

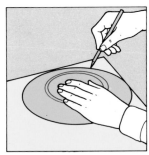

5. For intricate and irregular curves, make up a cardboard template or use a profile gauge

6. To draw ellipses use two pins, a loop of string and a pencil. Keep the string taut as you draw

Marking angles

Accurate marking of angles other than right angles is necessary for making certain woodworking joints, and you may need to cut other components at various angles to match existing hardware.

The commonest angle you'll need to mark is 45° – for miter joints and the like. The simplest way of marking this accurately is with a combination square, which will also mark right angles. If you already have a try square, buy a miter square, which resembles a try square but has the blade set at 45° to the stock.

For marking angles other than 45° you need a tool called a T-bevel. This has a fully adjustable blade secured to the stock with a wing nut. To set it accurately to a particular angle, you need a large protractor – small plastic school protractors are not really accurate enough. You can also use it to transfer the angle from an existing component to a new workpiece.

Marking dovetails is particularly tricky; use a special dovetail template for this.

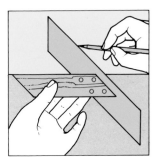

1. To mark a 45° angle with a combination square, press the angled stock against the edge

2. Use a miter square to mark 45° or 135° angles, and to test the accuracy of each cut component

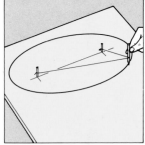

3. To mark any other angle, you need a T-bevel and protractor. Set the angle and lock

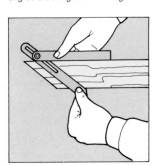

4. Use the T-bevel on its own to transfer an existing angle to a new workpiece

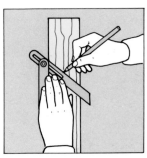

5. Check that the stock is firmly locked, then hold it against the face edge and mark the angle

6. Use a dovetail template to mark the pin positions on both components of a dovetail joint

119

Cutting a convex edge

If you want to cut a convex edge on a piece of wood by hand, you can use a crosscut saw in conjunction with a surform tool. Use the saw to make a straight cut across the corner to be removed, just on the waste side of the marked curve (see p. 119).

Make more cuts to create a series of shallow corners around the perimeter of the curve, then set the workpiece on edge in a vice and shave off the remaining waste to the marked profile.

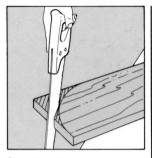

1. *Mark out the workpiece, clamp it flat and make a straight cut across the corner*

Using a coping or fret saw

To cut curves by hand in thin wood, a fine blade is needed. The coping saw has a metal frame and 6in long detachable blade with about 14 teeth per inch which point towards the handle. For finer work a fret saw is best: its blade, 5 to 6in long, is held tensioned in a deep frame.

Blades are detachable and can be passed through a pre-drilled hole, reconnected, and used to cut internal curves within reach of the frame.

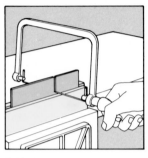

1. *If using a coping saw, support the workpiece both sides of the cutting line*

2. *Make more cuts, creating shallow corners around the length of the curve*

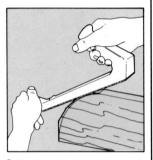

3. *Set the workpiece on edge and use a sharp-bladed surform tool to round off the curve*

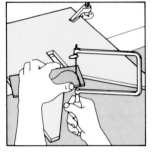

2. *With a fret saw, cuts are made vertically from below; a shaped platform allows access*

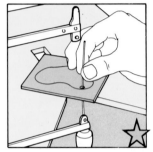

3. *For intricate curves, disconnect blade, pass through a drilled hole, then reconnect*

Using power tools

Even awkward curves in wood can be cut using power tools. The saber saw (see p. 125) is especially versatile – it can tackle softwoods up to 2¾in thick, hardwoods up to 1½in thick and most man-made boards: just guide the blade along the line.

To deal with extremely complex curves in thin woods – soft or hard – a powered fret saw offers greatest controllability: you guide the workpiece itself while the saw remains stationary.

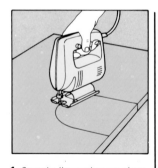

1. *Start the jigsaw then run along the marked line in one smooth, gentle motion*

Curving thick timber

If you want to cut a curve in timber that's too thick to tackle with a jigsaw, you can use a combination of sawing by hand, chiselling and planing.

Mark out the curve then clamp the workpiece in a vise or between bench stops and make a series of saw cuts down as far as the line, using a tenon saw.

Use a bevel-edged chisel and mallet to chop out the bulk of the waste. Finally, use a spokeshave to smooth the timber down to the curved line.

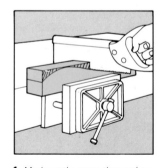

1. *Mark out the curve then make a series of tenon saw cuts as far as the line*

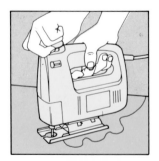

2. *One jigsaw features a knob allowing the blade to turn independently for tight curves*

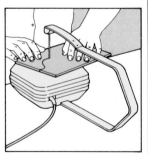

3. *A powered fret saw cuts with a vibrating blade onto which you guide the workpiece*

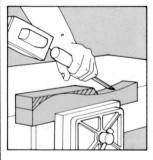

2. *Chop out most of the waste with a chisel and mallet, cutting down into the curve*

3. *Use a spokeshave to plane away the remaining waste to create a smooth curve*

Planing wood

Using a bench plane

A bench plane is basically a chisel blade mounted in a jig or holder, which is used to reduce the width or thickness of a piece of wood, smooth its surface and insure that the sides are at right angles to each other. There are various types of plane for different qualities of finish, but the jack plane is perhaps the best general purpose tool.

The plane comprises an iron body with a flat sole with a slot (mouth) through which the blade projects. There are handles front and back. The blade, or iron, is mounted with its cutting bevels facing down on a wedge-shaped component called the 'frog'; it's held secure by a cap iron and lever iron. A lever on the frog enables the iron to be aligned in the slot so it's parallel with the sole; a wheel-nut raises and lowers the blade, altering the amount protruding through the mouth, controlling the thickness of shaving. A screw enables the iron to be moved back and forth, altering the size of the mouth – this produces a finer finish but at a loss of cutting speed.

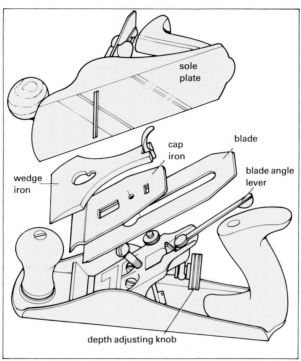

1. *The parts of a jack plane comprise body with handles, frog, which holds the iron, cap iron and lever cap in place, frog adjustment screws and blade adjustment wheel-nut*

2. *Sight along sole; adjust so the cutting edge is level and protrudes by less than 1/32in*

3. *Correct stance is important: hold the plane in both hands, body balanced above it*

4. *If you have a portable bench you can hold the wood between jaws or bench tops*

5. *To plane an edge press down on the front edge at the start with fingers supporting plane*

6. *During the cut, press down on both sides, then just the rear end as you finish*

7. *Keep plane square to the workpiece. You should produce a long, ribbon-like shaving*

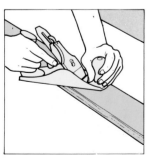

8. *When planing a wide board, angle the plane to reduce resistance; gradually straighten*

9. *To plane end grain, clamp the wood in a vice with an offcut to avoid splitting*

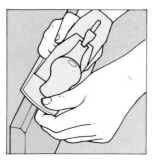

10. *Alternatively bevel all four corners then plane from one end to the middle*

11. *Make a 'shooting board' as a guide to planing edges or end grain squarely*

Radiusing and bevelling

Radiusing thin wood

If you don't want to make a flat bevel to finish an edge below you can put a radius on the edges of wood or manufactured sheets to soften the appearance. Because the line is less definite than a bevel or chamfer, you can afford to shape the radius by eye without being precise, but it's best to experiment first.

You could radius a thin edge with coarse sandpaper, followed by medium and fine held loosely in your hand, but you must try to keep a consistent shape.

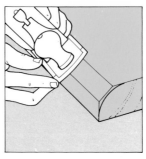

1. Mold a sheet of sandpaper into a concave curve. Run it along the edge for a mild radius

Radiusing thick wood

With thicker wood it's more likely you'll want a deeper and more pronounced radius, in which case it's more important that you be systematic. Experiment on an off-cut gain, but use it to make a template when you're satisfied.

Use the template to mark the ends of the wood – all eight corners if the workpiece is to be square or rectangular.

Plane a series of bevels on the edges as close to the curved lines as you can (below) then turn the bevels into a radius.

1. Use a curved template to mark the ends. Mark a bevel inside the waste area

2. *Cut a template from card or thin plywood to check the curve at various points*

3. *You could shape an offcut and wrap sandpaper around it to make a consistent radius on an edge*

2. *Scribe the face side and edge then plane a bevel down to the lines. Plane off the corners*

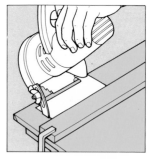

3. *Form the curve with sandpaper but use a template to check the shape at various points*

Bevelling with a plane

Cutting wood to an accurate bevel is not easy unless you have a definite guideline to follow. Set the angle precisely using a T-bevel and transfer it to both ends of the workpiece – make sure you slant it the correct way. Extend the depth along the wood with a marking gauge.

Cutting the bevel demands a steady hand and keen eye: hold the plane at the correct angle and steady it with the fingers of one hand. Plane smoothly and evenly from the shoulder.

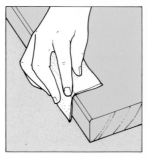

1. Set a T-bevel to the angle you want, then scribe a mark on each end of the wood

Power saw bevelling

The easiest way to cut bevels is to use a power circular or saber saw. Many models have adjustable sole plates, which tilt.

Circular saws have a gauge attached to the sole plate, for setting precise angles.

Clamp the wood flat on a work-bench or table with the edge to be bevelled overhanging by about 3in. On long lengths, use a fence to guide the blade; if the saw has no fence, clamp a board to the work-piece parallel with the edge

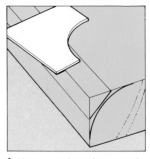

1. Set the sole plate of a power saw to the angle required for the bevel you want

2. *Set a marking gauge to the depth of the bevel and the scribe along the face and edge*

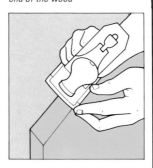

3. *Set the wood in a vise and plane along the edge at an angle until you reach the lines*

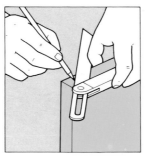

2. *Clamp the wood to a bench so that the marked out edge overhangs the edge of the bench*

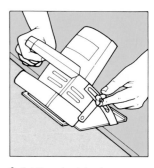

3. *Run the saw along the timber following a fence or using a straightedge as a cutting guide*

Scribing to fit

Scribing to depth

Once you have scribed and cut the shelf panel to fit across the width of the alcove, you need to do likewise with the back edge, where the shelf butts up against the back wall.

With the shelf in position, it's easy enough to scribe the back edge of the panel to fit the profile of the alcove wall.

If the alcove is virtually square, there's no need to cut the shelf to any intricate profile; you can simply butt it up to the wall (so long as the front edge of the shelf is square within the alcove). Insure this by cutting the front edge to fit after you've scribed and cut the back edge.

To scribe the back edge of the shelf panel to fit you'll need a pencil and a block of wood, which you can use as a spacer; check that the front edge is flush with the front wall by holding a straight-edged length of wood across both.

You can use the same method for scribing vertical panels of wall panelling – tongued-and-grooved boarding and man-made boards, for instance.

1. *Slot the shelf panel into the recess and butt it up tightly against the back wall*

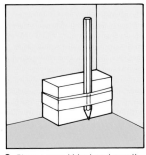

2. *Place a wood block and pencil on the shelf, butt it up to the back wall at one side*

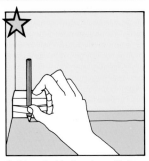

3. *Draw the block and pencil along the back wall, scribing the profile on the shelf*

4. *Saw along the guideline using a saber saw then push the shelf into the back wall*

5. *Set the shelf flush with the front walls of the alcove by aligning with a straightedge*

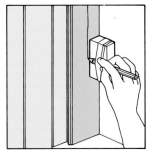

6. *With wall panelling, butt the panel against the adjacent wall; scribe with block and pencil*

Scribing to width

Alcoves are rarely truly square and when you're fitting a shelf in an alcove you'll probably experience difficulties in getting a good fit. You could fill minor gaps with a flexible filler but any substantial irregularity should be cut into the shape of the shelf materials.

The secret is to scribe each panel individually to fit the profile of the alcove and then to saw along the guideline. Use a saber saw for this: the tool is able to follow modest curves and it's unlikely that the alcove will be so untrue that you will need to cut complex curves. For small irregularities, use a plane or surform tool to remove the waste.

Aim to measure the width of the alcove at three points – back, center and front – then transfer these dimensions to the uncut shelf material, which may be man-made boards or solid wood planks.

On a narrow alcove, you can take the measurements using a steel tape measure, but for a wider recess you will need to improvise an extendable gauge using thin softwood strips.

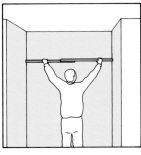

1. *Hold two slim strips together with a slight overlap so they span the full width of the alcove*

2. *Scribe a line across both strips with a pencil; you can now separate them*

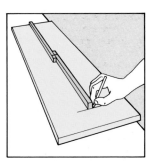

3. *Place the strips on the shelf and align the pencil marks, then mark off at the ends*

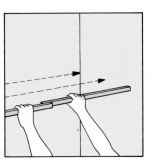

4. *Repeat the measuring at the middle and front of the alcove to plot the wall's profile*

5. *Join up the marks to give the profile of the alcove walls, using a ruler and pencil*

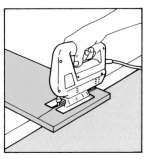

6. *Saw along the guidelines using a saber saw to cut the shelf to width*

Drilling holes in wood (electric drill)

Drilling techniques

Correct stance, grip on the drill and careful operation of the tool are necessary when drilling. Stand well-balanced and grip the handle of the drill in your right hand, the body – just behind the chuck – with your left (vice versa if you're left-handed).

Before you start to drill, punch an indent in the wood at the marked hole position using a center punch, or make a starter hole with a bradawl; this is to prevent the drill bit skidding.

Drill slowly, withdrawing the bit periodically to expel sawdust from the threads. Never force the bit: it will bind in the hole and may snap. It's worth taking stock of how vertically you're drilling – keep check with a try square.

You should be able to feel when the drill bit breaks through the wood; when this happens, don't release the trigger or the bit will be held firmly in the hole. Keep it running and withdraw the bit cleanly.

On thick lumber, mark out both sides accurately, drill as deep as possible then complete the hole from the other side of the wood.

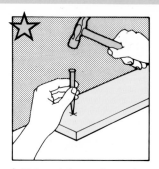

1. Make an indent on the wood with a punch or bradawl to stop the drill bit wandering

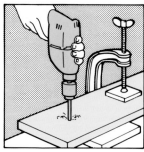

2. Drill through, periodically withdrawing to expel sawdust. Withdraw bit with drill running

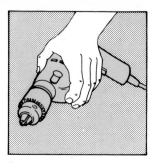

3. Some electric drills have a reverse action to make withdrawal easier and cleaner

4. You should feel the bit break through; double-check with a depth stop though

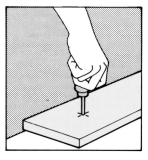

5. If the bit smokes during drilling, it needs changing, sharpening or tightening in the chuck

6. On thick lumber it's best to drill from both sides, accurate marking and drilling is vital

Setting up to drill

If you're drilling a fixed unit, you only need to insure that you drill at a right-angle: hold a try square at the side to check.

Hold a loose workpiece with C-clamps. To stop the bit from splitting the wood as it emerges at the other side (and to protect the surface you're working on) clamp the wood over scrap wood; scraps under the clamp jaws will protect the wood.

Mark the hole position on the wood; use a bradawl to make an indent to stop the bit wandering.

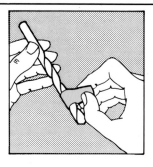

1. Mark the position of the hole with a cross, then indent the mark with a bradawl

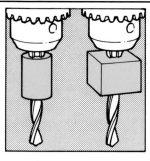

2. Clamp the workpiece over an offcut of wood, with scrap pieces under the clamp jaws

3. Hold the drill at right angles to the wood and use a try square to check the vertical

Drilling to depth

To drill to the correct depth to take a screw or dowel, use a simple guide to insure accuracy. Chalk the bit the required distance from its tip, or wind adhesive tape round it. When this reaches the wood, you know you've drilled far enough.

A more accurate method is to use a proprietary device that can be fixed anywhere on the bit.

You can make your own stop from a large dowel; drill a hole through it, cut it to length and slot it onto the bit.

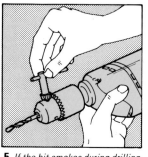

1. Wind a piece of adhesive tape around the drill bit and use the 'flag' as a depth guide

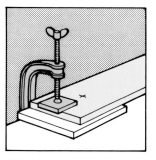

2. A drilled dowel or offcut slotted on the bit can be used as a depth guide and stop

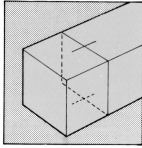

3. A brand-name depth stop and guide allows you to adjust the depth you drill to

Using a saber saw

Setting up the saber saw

The saber saw is at it's best used for cornered and curved cuts in softwoods up to 2¾in thick, hardwoods up to 1½in thick and virtually any man-made boards.

Saber saw blades are straight and narrow, 3 to 4in long, and move up and down through a sole plate, cutting on the upstroke, for thin wood you need a fine blade with closely-spaced teeth; for thicker wood a coarser blade with fewer teeth at wider spacings is best.

How to use the saber saw

A saber saw is portable, easy to use and versatile enough to cut fairly tight curves, angular cut-outs and straight lines – although the result can be a bit wobbly (the blade tends to wander) unless you use a fence to guide it along a straight line. Some saber saws come with an integral fence to cope with modest widths, although you can rig up your own guide for cuts down the center of a wide sheet.

The sole plate can be angled on some saber saws.

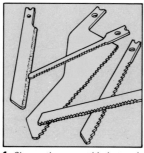

1. *Choose the correct blade to suit the material for coarse, fine or curved cuts*

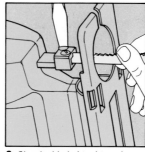

2. *Slot the blade into its socket and tighten the integral retaining screw to secure it*

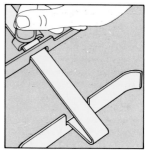

3. *Set the fence to keep the same distance between the cutting line and the edge of the wood*

4. *On some saws the sole plate can be tilted and locked to produce a bevelled cut*

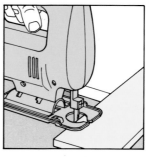

5. *With a bevelling facility, its best to make a test cut on scrap wood to check the angle.*

6. *Stick tape over the cutting line on veneered/laminated surfaces to prevent splitting*

1. *Place a try square on a narrow workpiece as a visual guide to sawing squarely*

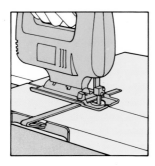

2. *Run the fence along the edge of the wood on long cuts to give a straight line*

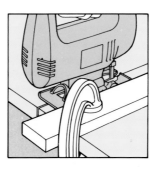

3. *For cuts in a wide sheet clamp a 1 × 2 to the surface and run the sole plate along it*

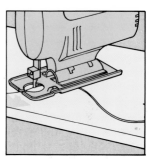

4. *Guide the saw blade along a curved cutting line in one continuous motion*

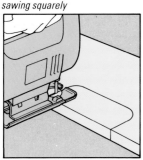

5. *To cut a notch: run blade in at each side, reverse, curve corner then remove waste*

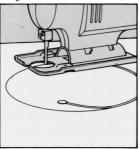

6. *For a cut-out, drill holes for the blade at the perimeter, cut between them to remove waste*

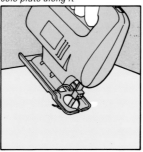

7. *To plunge-cut, rest front of sole plate on wood, switch on and ease in the blade*

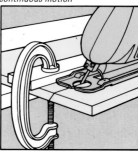

8. *Set the sole plate to the required bevel or miter. Cut against a fence*

Using a router

Types of router

A power router is used to cut grooves, chamfers, rabbets, bevels and other decorative shapes in wood. The tool basically comprises a high-speed motor (up to around 30,000rpm, as opposed to a power drill's 3000rpm), which drives a revolving shaft fitted with a chuck (called a collet) into which the cutter is fixed.

There are basically two types of router. With the fixed-base type, the cutter protrudes permanently from the baseplate at a pre-set depth; with the plunging type – the simplest to use – the motor is mounted on a spring-loaded mechanism, which allows the cutter to be lowered to pre-set depths.

Plunging router

To use the plunging router, you simply position where required, switch on then press down on the handles to plunge the rotating cutter into the wood. Running the tool along the workpiece forms the cut, although pocket cuts in the middle of the workpiece can be made. Fixed fences give accurate cuts parallel to an edge.

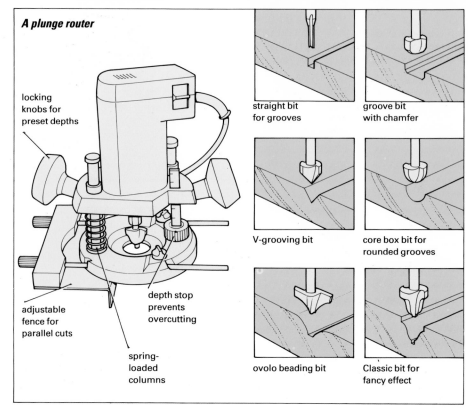

A plunge router

locking knobs for preset depths

adjustable fence for parallel cuts

spring-loaded columns

depth stop prevents overcutting

straight bit for grooves

groove bit with chamfer

V-grooving bit

core box bit for rounded grooves

ovolo beading bit

Classic bit for fancy effect

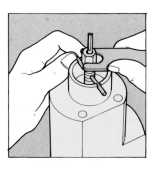

1. *Remove the motor from the housing; fit the cutter in the collet; tighten with a wrench*

2. *Replace the motor in the carriage and secure it by tightening its knob*

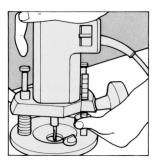

3. *Set the depth of cut you want and secure the carriage by turning the grip knob*

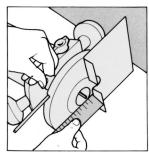

4. *For parallel cuts, fit a fence to the base of the router and set at distance required*

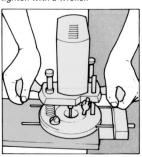

5. *Place the router on the workpiece, switch on then press the handles to plunge the cutter*

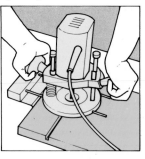

6. *When the cutter reaches full depth, twist the handle to lock and run the tool along the wood*

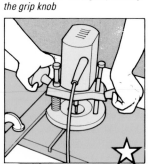

7. *For cutting in the middle of a workpiece, clamp a straightedge to it and use as a fence*

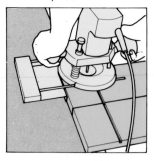

8. *Use an overshoot board to support an adjustable fence at end of cut, avoiding splintering*

Making butt joints

Marking and cutting

The butt joint is the basic way to join two components; it can be used on any solid or man-made board over ¼in thick.

The simplest joint is to butt and glue the end of one onto the face of its partner but reinforcement is usually added (see right). The marking out and cutting techniques are similar for all: of prime importance is insuring that the meeting faces are precisely square. Use a bench hook to help you grip the wood and saw straight and even.

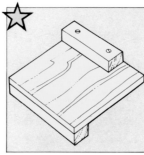

1. Make a bench hook from an offcut with cleats screwed on opposite sides at each end

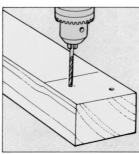

2. Hold the wood on the hook, make two backward cuts, saw angled, then decrease the angle

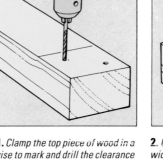

3. Bring the pieces together squarely and mark the position of each on its partner

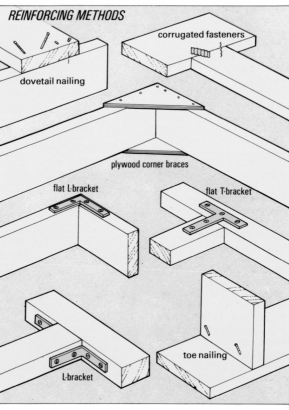

REINFORCING METHODS

corrugated fasteners

dovetail nailing

plywood corner braces

flat L-bracket

flat T-bracket

L-bracket

toe nailing

Overlap butt joint

The overlapping butt joint is the easiest to make for T-joints, L-joints and cross joints. When reinforced with screws, it's fairly strong and neat.

Mark out the components accurately with a pencil and try square (see p. 118) and cut to length with a tenon saw, holding the wood in a bench hook (see overleaf).

Piece together the components as they will be joined – support the rear end of the top piece on an offcut – and mark their positions on each other, then drill the screw holes.

Use countersunk screws for strength, arranged on the wood like dice spots. For wood up to about 2 × 3in in section, two screws are adequate; for thicker lumber five are better, so the joint won't twist.

Choose the correct size screw for the thickness of wood and drill clearance holes through the top component to take them. Drill or bore pilot holes in the bottom piece through the clearance holes of the top one.

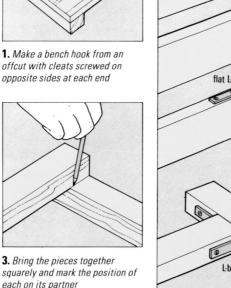

1. Clamp the top piece of wood in a vise to mark and drill the clearance holes

2. Use a countersinking bit to widen the mouths of the holes to recess the screw heads

3. Assemble the pieces and bore pilot holes in the lower one with a bradawl or drill bit

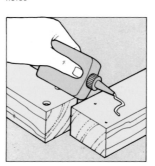

4. Smear PVA adhesive on the meeting faces and assemble the components accurately

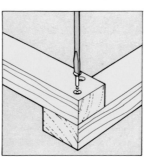

5. Drive in screws squarely, wipe off smears and set aside for the adhesive to dry

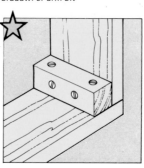

6. Reinforce a right-angled butt joint with a wood block screwed into the corner

Making dowel joints

Marking out the joints

A dowel joint is a butt-joint strengthened by short lengths of cylindrical dowel glued in predrilled holes in the mating faces of each component.

Pre-cut hardwood dowels are sold in packs in various diameters and lengths. The dowels are fluted along their length to allow excess adhesive to escape, and are chamfered at each end to make fitting easier.

Uncut dowel lengths in a wider range of diameters are sold by lumber yards, but for simple projects pre-cut types are best.

When making a dowel joint, it's vital that the dowels are inserted perfectly squarely in the holes or the two pieces of wood won't butt up correctly.

Precise marking out is essential and for this you'll need a try square, marking gauge, a pencil and either some small wire brads or dowel centers. You'll also need some pliers for withdrawing the brads.

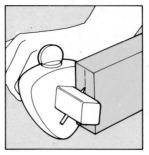

1. *Set a marking gauge to half the wood thickness and scribe along the end of one piece*

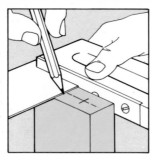

2. *Divide the line into three, draw two lines at right-angles at the outer divisions*

3. *Tap in small wire brads at these points; snip off their heads so ⅛in protrudes*

4. *Hold the mating piece in the angle of a try square and the other piece at right-angles*

5. *Push the pinned end against the side of the mating piece to mark the drill holes*

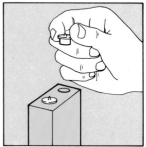

6. *Alternatively, drill shallow holes and insert dowel centers to mark the abutting component*

Drilling the dowel holes

The holes to take the dowels must be drilled perfectly squarely or the joint won't align. You can drill the holes free-hand (using a try square as a guide), but you risk the bit wandering off course, so it's easiest to use a dowelling jig – the device clamps onto the workpiece as a guide.

So you don't drill too shallow or too deep a hole, make a simple depth guide by winding adhesive tape around the bit.

Use a dowel bit the same diameter as the dowel

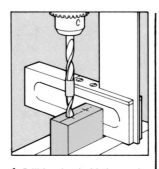

1. *Drill free-hand with the wood clamped in a vise and a try square as a guide to level*

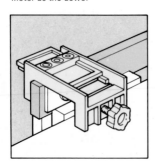

2. *Clamp a dowelling jig to the wood, using scrap wood to protect the face*

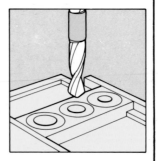

3. *Insert the drill bit in the correct size hole of the jig and drill to the required depth*

Fitting the dowels

Assemble the joint dry to make sure that it is accurately square before you apply glue. Check also that the holes are drilled slightly deeper than the dowel's length, in case of excess adhesive.

It's a good idea for easing the assembly of the dowel joints to slightly recess the mouths of the dowel holes, using a countersinking bit.

Use PVA woodworking adhesive for gluing in the dowels, then clamp the joint until it is completely dry.

1. *Daub PVA adhesive onto one half of the pre-cut dowel, using an old paintbrush*

2. *Insert the dowel in the hole and tap it in gently and squarely with a mallet*

3. *Apply adhesive to the protruding ends of the dowels and slot on the mating piece*

Making halving joints

Corner halving joints

The corner halving joint is a simple but strong joint for all sorts of frameworks. Its strength comes from the fact that the two components interlock, providing a sizeable area for the adhesive bond. The end result is a joint that has both components flush with one another, with just a small area of end grain exposed on each side of the corner. Provided that the joint is cut neatly and accurately, the only reinforcement needed is adhesive – PVA woodworking adhesive for normal work, a urea formaldehyde resin adhesive for outdoors.

If extra reinforcement is needed, you can drive screws through the overlaps or drill through them and drive in glued dowels. Use two positioned diagonally on the overlap area.

When marking out the joints, always use actual rather than the nominal size, and mark cutting lines with a knife rather than a pencil. Cross-hatch all waste areas in pencil and when making a series, label matching components – eg A1 and A2 – as you cut them.

1. First mark the width of each piece on the end of the other, using a marking knife

2. Check that the line is square, then continue it down onto the two sides of each piece

3. Set your marking gauge to half the wood thickness and scribe a line on both edges

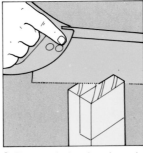

4. Clamp each piece in a vise and saw at an angle on the waste side. Finish the cut with the blade horizontal

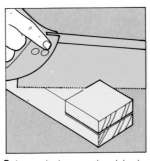

5. Lay each piece on a bench hook and saw down the width line. Cut on the waste side

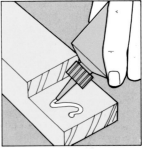

6. Test the two parts for fit, and adjust if necessary. Then apply adhesive to one component

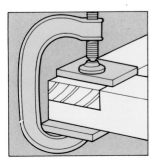

7. Use a C-clamp and packing pieces to clamp the joint securely until the adhesive has dried

Cross halving joints

Where the two components meet in a T or X rather than an L, a notch has to be cut in one (T) or both (X) components. As with a corner halving joint, use one component of the joint to mark the width of the cut-out on the other. Then saw down to the depth lines on the notched piece and remove the waste with a sharp chisel. Pare away a little more wood from each component if necessary to get a tight fit. Finally knock the parts apart, glue the overlap and reassemble.

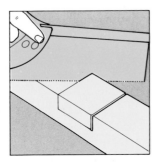

1. When you've marked out the piece to be notched, saw down to the depth line at each side

2. Hold the wood in a vise and chisel up towards the center from the depth line at each side

8. If necessary, reinforce the joint with two countersunk screws or wood dowels

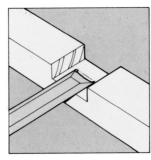

3. Gradually flatten the 'pyramid' of waste from both sides until the cut-out has a flat base

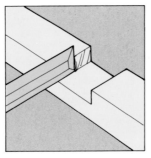

4. Trim the sides of the notch with a sharp chisel if the two components are a tight fit

5. Finally apply adhesive to one surface, assemble the joint with a mallet and clamp until dry

Making miter joints

Marking and cutting joints

Miter joints are made to form a 90° angle between two pieces of wood; it's not a strong means of joining wood – little more than a butt joint – but is suitable for neatness in picture framing or in making a door casing or decorative edging because it leaves no exposed end-grain.

Basic miter joints can be cut in square- or rectangular-section wood using only a try square, marking knife and tenon saw, holding the pieces on a bench hook. In molded wood that's raised on one side – picture frame sections, for instance – you'll need the assistance and accuracy of a miter box in order to support the piece while you make the cut: this is simply a U-shaped assembly with saw guides on the sides that give 45° or 90° cuts when the workpiece is held inside. Brand-name jointing jigs are available, which allow you to cut and assemble miter joints easily.

Beware of cutting two right- or left-handed miters on molded wood instead of one of each – an important point if you're making a profiled-section frame.

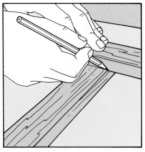

1. Stack square or rectangular wood at right-angles; mark inner and outer corners on both

2. Carry the lines down each edge with a trimming knife held against a try square

3. Score a line between the corner marks, giving an angle of 45°. Cross-hatch the waste

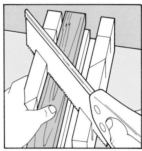

4. Hold the piece in a miter box, align with the guides, then cut with a tenon saw

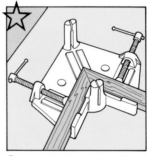

5. A jointing jig can be used to cut accurate miters and hold the pieces when glued

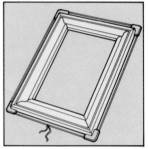

6. A store-bought string clamp will hold a miter-jointed frame securely until set

Assembling a miter joint

In order for the meeting faces of the miter joint to connect squarely, it's necessary to plane the ends after cutting to remove burrs – but beware of radiusing or distorting the edges.

The most basic miter joint can simply be assembled using just PVA woodworking adhesive, but it's not particularly strong and only suitable for lightweight frames, or where the components themselves are secured to a base (a casement nailed to a door frame, for instance).

For stronger attachments you can adopt one of the illustrated methods – corrugated connectors, metal repair brackets and plywood triangles can be used behind the frame for a concealed fixing; dowels, nails and halving joints provide the neatest and strongest joining method for decorative woodwork.

In either case, apply the adhesive to meeting faces, bring together and secure as required. Clamp in a jointing jig or miter clamp, or use a string clamp on a frame making sure you keep the frame square.

1. Glue the pieces together and strengthen with brads, heads sunk below the surface

2. With thick wood, hammer corrugated steel fasteners into the back of the joint

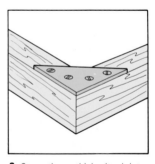

3. Strengthen a thick miter joint with plywood triangles fixed across the corners

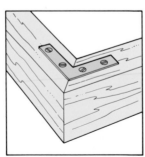

4. Flat metal angle brackets can be used to give a rigid fixing for mitered cleats

5. Dowels provide one of the neatest and strongest fixings for mitering two components

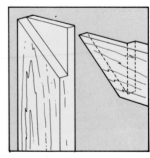

6. A halving joint restores the original thickness and strength of the wood

Making housing joints

Through housing joints

Housing joints are used in the construction of cabinets, shelf units, drawers, door frames and in stud partition wall, where they're both strong (resisting twisting) and neat (no brackets are required in assembly).

The basic through housing joint is made by recessing one component (a shelf for instance) into a square-bottomed channel cut in another (an upright, for example). To make the joint, just mark the position of the first piece on the piece to be routed, cut down the sides of the housing with a tenon saw to one-third its thickness then pare out the waste wood with a suitably wide bevel-edged chisel.

For short housings it's best to set the workpiece on edge on scrap wood and chisel out of the waste vertically for accuracy.

To make short work of cutting the housing, you can use a power router, which eliminates sawing and chiselling; a circular saw can be used likewise, although you'll need to make several overlapping slices to remove the bulk of the waste.

1. *A plain through housing consists of one board recessed into a channel in another*

2. *Scribe across the inner face of the housing piece with a knife against a try square*

3. *Measure the width of the shelf piece and scribe this dimension on the other piece*

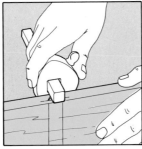

4. *Set a marking gauge to ⅓ the wood thickness and scribe on the upright's edges*

5. *Use a knife against a try square to square the housing sides on the upright's edges*

6. *Lie the upright flat and saw along the housing edges, then centrally between cuts*

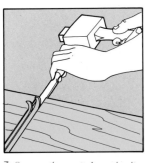

7. *Remove the waste by paring it out carefully with a chisel the width of the housing*

8. *Use the cut housing to mark the position of the channel on the opposite upright*

Barefaced and stopped housings

There are two basic variations on the plain through housing joint, used for decorative but, more important, concealed joints in cabinet-making.

The stopped housing joint is invisible: the inset piece is stopped short of the front of the routed piece by about ¾in; it's also possible to cut a notch out of the front corners of the inset piece so that its leading edge will sit flush with the front of the connecting piece.

A barefaced housing joint is usually used at the corner of an assembly, where an ordinary housing can't be cut: the end of the inset piece has a step or rabbet cut across its width, forming a narrow tongue, which slots into a correspondingly narrower housing in the adjoining piece.

You can also use this joint with the rabbet on an upright, let into a housing in the underside of a horizontal, so you have an unbroken line of wood grain along the top. The barefaced housing joint is good at keeping the structure rigid.

1. *The barefaced housing joint is used at corners where a plain housing can't be cut*

9. *Place a straightedge in the base of the channel to make sure that the housing is level*

10. *Apply glue to the meeting faces of the housing joint and secure with nails*

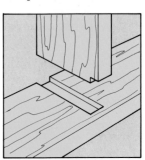

2. *A stopped housing with shoulder provides an invisible joint with a neat finish*

Fitting butt hinges

Fitting the hinges

Butt hinges are the commonest types for room and full-height cupboard doors. They comprise two brass, steel, cast iron or nylon flaps – with three or more pre-drilled countersunk screw holes – attached by a fixed or loose pin at the knuckle: rising butts have a spiral knuckle which enables the door to rise as it opens to clear a carpet, and allows the door to be lifted off.

The rectangular flaps are usually recessed into the door edge and frame, although it is possible to surface-mount them. Hinge sizes range from 1in for furniture to over 4in for room doors.

When fitting butt hinges, each one must line up vertically and be recessed flush with the door edge, or the door may bind and the hinges will be strained.

The first part of the job is to fit the hinges to the door edge. To fit them you'll need a try square, marking gauge, bevel-edged chisel (1in for room doors), an electric drill and twist bit, plus a screwdriver.

1. Mark the hinge positions on the door edge and square the lines across with a try square

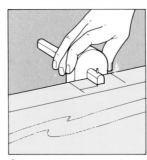

2. Set a marking gauge to the width and depth of the flap; scribe between the lines

3. Chop out the hinge flap recesses to the correct depth using a bevel-edged chisel

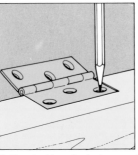

4. Test the hinge flap in the recess and adjust until it's flush. Mark the screw holes

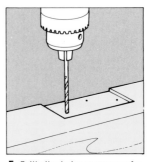

5. Drill pilot holes as starters for the fixing screws, using a small diameter twist bit

6. Attach the hinges with flathead screws; heads should be flush with the flap

Hanging the door

The trickiest part of hanging a door with butt hinges is to position it squarely within the frame: the hinge flap recesses must not be cut too deeply, or in the wrong places.

Wedge the door in the frame with a small gap all round it so it won't bind; with a large door, use triangular offcuts of wood, with a cupboard door pieces of card or hardboard should do.

Mark out the positions of the hinges on the frame then transfer the marks onto the face of the jamb using a marking gauge set to the width of the flaps. You'll need a bevel-edged chisel to chop out the recesses to the same depth as the flap thickness, though you may need to adjust.

If you do cut the recesses too deep and the door binds on the hinge side, cut rectangles of hardboard (card for small doors) and tack them in the cutout. If the door binds on the other side, cut deeper recesses.

When a door swings open or shut of its own accord, the hinge flaps aren't set vertically: realign them accordingly.

1. Wedge the door within the frame and mark the hinge positions on the frame's face

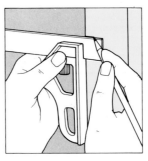

2. Square the hinge positions on the side of the frame and mark the width of the recesses

3. Cut the recesses to the flap thickness using a bevel-edged chisel; don't cut too deep

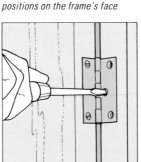

4. Prop up the door adjacent to the frame, hinges aligned with recesses; fix with one screw

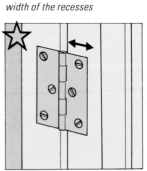

5. If the door swings open, reposition the hinge on the frame to one side accordingly

6. If the door binds on its hinge side, the recesses are too deep; nail on hardboard shims

Fitting flush, cranked & piano hinges

Cranked lift-off hinges

Cranked hinges are used on light-weight doors – typically kitchen cabinets or wardrobes – where it's necessary for the door to open within its own width: where the cabinet abuts a wall or is in a row of cabinets.

One leaf of a cranked hinge is bent into a right-angle: the door fits within the angle. Although the hinge is basically like a butt hinge (see p. 132), the pivot position is brought forward to the front of the cabinet instead of being sandwiched between door and carcase. You're also able to fix into the face of a man-made material such as wallboard rather than the edge, which gives firmer fixing.

Double cranked hinges have both leaves bent at right-angles, which makes them useful for a wardrobe containing drawers, where extra door clearance is needed to open the drawers. The screw fixings are made in both edges and faces.

Lift-off cranked hinges enable you to fit the leaves separately so you don't have to prop the door while you screw the hinges.

1. *Use a marking gauge to score a line indicating the hinge flap position on the door face*

2. *Cut recesses for the flaps on the inner face of the door with a bevel-edged chisel*

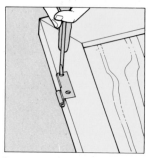
3. *Screw the top half of the hinge – with the socket – to the recess on the door*

4. *Screw the other leaf of the hinge onto the carcase edge, spindle upwards*

5. *Lift the door onto the cabinet, slotting the socket onto the spindle*

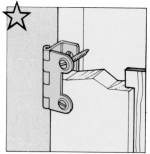
6. *Surface mount double cranked hinges on the face and edge of door and frame*

Fitting flush hinges

Flush hinges are a type of butt hinge in which a small flap attached to the door closes within, rather than against, a larger one fixed to the frame.

Suitable only for lightweight fold-away doors, inset doors or screens, they don't require recesses to be cut: when the door is shut, the gap between it and the carcase is the thickness of the hinge flaps.

To fit the hinges, attach them to the door edge first, then to the cabinet frame.

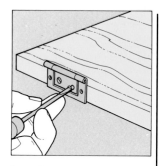
1. *Mark the hinge positions on the door against a try square then screw on the small flap*

2. *Hold the door against the frame and mark off the hinge positions; bore the screw holes*

3. *With the door propped in place, screw on the large hinge flaps, aligning the knuckles*

Fitting a piano hinge

Piano (or continuous) butt hinges are sold in lengths up to about 6ft and can be cut to size with a hacksaw. Leaves are slimmer than on other butt hinges, so they give a rigid fixing on doors no thicker than ½in.

Usually brass or nickel-plated steel hinges are also made in white finish (some in plastic). Attachment holes are spaced wider apart than other hinges – about 2 ¾in – so when you cut, insure there's a hole near each end for a firm attachment.

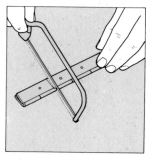
1. *Saw a piano hinge to length using a hacksaw: insure there's a fixing near each end*

2. *Screw the piano hinge to the full length of the door edge, making sure it's aligned*

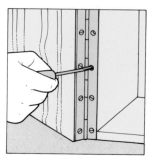
3. *Prop the door against the side of the cabinet and secure the free flap to the edge*

Using concealed spring hinges

Recessed concealed hinges

Concealed hinges are extensively used for fixing doors on panel furniture. The device is hidden within the cabinet and enables the door to open within the width of the cabinet so it won't foul on adjacent doors.

Different versions open the door at various angles – 90° and 110° – for access. Some open to 170°, so the door folds flat if walked into. Others are spring-loaded, so no catch is required to keep the door shut. Lay-on and recessed types are made.

A 95°-opening recessed concealed hinge is the basic type. It's suitable for base and wall units. The base plate is in two parts – it has a screw adjustment for levelling the door.

A 110°-opening hinge is ideal for cupboards fitted with drawers – the door will not bind against the drawers.

A 170°-opening hinge opens a cabinet door fully and lifts it clear of adjacent doors too.

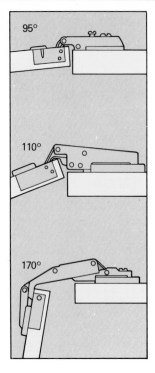

1. There are three basic types to choose from, depending on your kitchen layout

Fitting a concealed hinge

Lay-on concealed hinges are made, but the recessed type is most versatile, offering alignment after fitting. The device comprises a round hinge boss, which is fitted into a large 1½in diameter hole drilled in the inner face of the door with an end mill attachment to an electric drill (often pre-drilled in the door).

The arm of the hinge is screwed to the side panel of the carcase over a baseplate, which enables fine screw-operated alignments in all directions.

A second, small-diameter hole may be needed next to the boss hole, to take a short stub which prevents the boss from being pulled out of alignment, even though it's screwed into the stopped milled hole.

Baseplates are normally bought separately, as different types are required depending on the thickness of the door and the side panel to which you're attaching it: the plate effectively thickens the carcase. Basically, the thicker the door, the thicker the carcase must be – check when you buy the hinge.

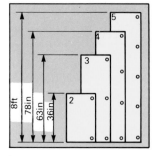

1. The number of hinges you need depends on the height of the cabinet door

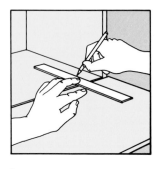

2. Mark the hole position on the door, plus the center line of the baseplate

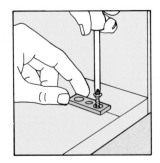

3. Mill a hole (depth depends on hinge) ⅛in from door edge, using a drill stand

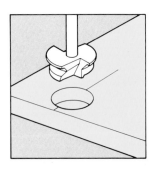

4. Drill any locating hole, push the boss in the recess and secure with screws

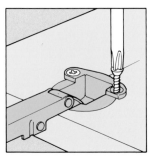

5. Position the baseplate on the guideline and mark the fixing holes on the carcase

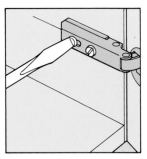

6. Screw the baseplate to the inner face of the carcase according to the fixings

7. Lift the door into place and screw the arms of the hinges to the baseplate

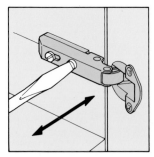

8. By slackening the relevant screw on the hinge arm, move the door in and out

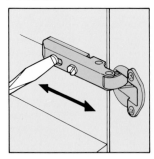

9. Correct sideways alignment by loosening a second screw, height is also adjustable

Applying wax, oil and lacquer

Finishing with wax

Wax is a traditional method of finishing wooden furniture and the most commonly used is beeswax, although carnauba, cerestine and paraffin waxes are also popular. You can prepare each type yourself and apply it to new wood to give a lustrous sheen – to achieve a workable substance it's usual to mix beeswax with one of the other waxes and an equal part of turpentine.

Shred the waxes (with a chisel or cheese grater) and mix them together. Then add the turpentine and melt the waxes by immersing them in a boil-proof jar in a pan of boiling water. When liquefied, you can add more beeswax and turpentine to provide sufficient quantity.

Once melted again then cooled, the wax (which should last indefinitely) can be scrubbed into wood grain with a bristle brush, left for 24 hours then burnished with steel wool. A final buff with a soft cloth produces an attractive sheen. By repeating the process every other day for a month or so the luster will develop.

1. Grate enough carnauba wax to fill two teaspoons; add similarly grated beeswax

2. Add the waxes to a boil-proof jar plus two teaspoonsful of turpentine, then stir

3. Lower the jar into a pan of boiling water and simmer until the contents have melted

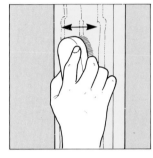

4. Apply the cooled mixture of waxes by scrubbing across the wood grain with a shoe brush

5. After 24 hours, burnish along the grain using 000 grade steel wool

6. Buff the waxed surface with a soft cloth; repeat process every other day over a month

Applying teak or Danish oil

It takes considerable time and patience to achieve depth of finish with oils, although application is easy. Traditionally, linseed oil was used but careful preparation is needed; teak or Danish oil is a good equivalent.

Prepare the wood by sealing then sanding with fine sandpaper. The oil is rubbed along the grain with a cloth pad then rubbed well in with 360–400 grit silicon carbide paper or 000 grade steel wool. After about three applications, buff with a soft cloth.

1. Rub teak oil along the wood grain with a cloth pad until it floods the surface

Finishing with lacquer

Lacquer provides a delicate sheen to wood, either colored or clear. It comes in cans or aerosols.

Work in a well-ventilated room and wear a facemask and rubber gloves (use lacquer thinner for cleaning). Don't attempt to brush on lacquer: it must be sprayed for a good finish using an air-driven gun with a pressure of over 70lb p.s.i.; the material must be mixed with thinner in equal proportions.

1. Spray lacquer from an aerosol in a forward direction 1ft from the surface

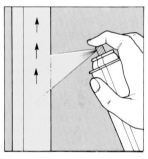

2. Wipe off excess oil after a few minutes then leave the surface to dry thoroughly

3. Smooth surface between coats by rubbing along the grain with abrasive paper

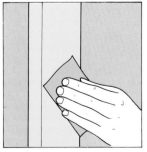

2. Smooth the surface with finishing paper after the first coat then repeat several times

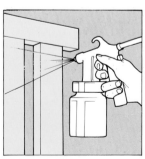

3. A rented spray gun is best for a fine finish. Always work in a well-ventilated room

French polishing wood

Applying shellac

Traditional French polishing is an art but you can approximate the characteristic mirror-like finish using one of the brand-name kits on the market. The surface of the wood itself must be free of marks, grease, dust and dirt.

With these kits – a bottle of shellac for the body of the polish and one of burnishing liquid – the first coats of polish can be applied by an ordinary paintbrush to fill the grain, and rubbed with extra-fine silicon carbide paper to remove blemishes.

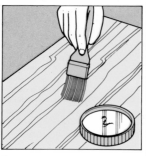

1. Apply an even coat of shellac to the wood in the direction of the grain; don't over-coat

2. Apply a second coat of shellac after 30 minutes. After 60 minutes sand with silicon carbide paper

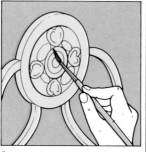

3. Use a fine artist's paintbrush to apply shellac to carved wood and thin components of furniture

Making a rubber

The body of the shellac is built up using a 'rubber'. This consists of a 12in square of white cotton rag, which has been soaked in wood alcohol then wrung out; a square of absorbent cotton is folded, soaked in shellac then wrapped in the rag.

The rag, twisted to provide a firm, flat-faced, wrinkle-free rubber, is drawn along the wood to discharge the shellac. Make two rubbers and keep one soaking in a jar of alcohol, exchanging it when the other clogs.

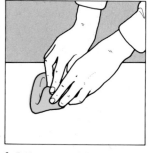

1. Fold a square of absorbent cotton into a tight, round-faced wad to act as the core of the rubber

2. Place the wad in the center of the cotton rag then pour some shellac into the core until moist

3. Fold the rag around the wad then twist the ends to make a firm, smooth-faced rubber

Applying French polish

Work in a warm room, as a cool atmosphere can cloud the polish, and in good light so that you can see the effect you're producing. Start applying the shellac by running the fully-charged rubber lightly along the wood in continuous circular motions. Keep the rubber moving all the time – if you hesitate a blemish will result – sweeping is smoothly off edges and back on again. Repeat the process about a dozen times.

Run the rubber in straight parallel strokes along the wood grain then apply another layer of shellac (with a recharged rubber) using figure-eight strokes to completely cover the surface.

Repeat the entire sequence until you achieve the depth of color you want, then allow to harden overnight.

Burnishing the polish

Finish the surface by dampening a wad of cotton wool in the burnishing liquid, then rub – quite hard – along the grain in a small area. Buff with a soft duster then move on to the adjoining area.

1. Draw the charged rubber along the workpiece in light, continuous circular motions

2. When you reach the edge, sweep the rubber off and back on again for another pass

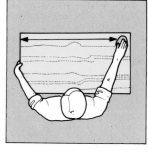

3. After several circular passes, run the rubber along the grain in sweeping parallel strokes

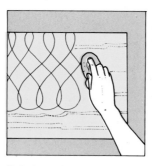

4. Recharge the rubber then apply the polish to the workpiece using figure-eight strokes

5. Burnish the polish when hard using absorbent cotton dampened with fluid; treat small areas at a time

6. Use a soft duster to produce the final highly glossy shine then move on to subsequent sections

Studs in a partition wall

If you're fixing units to a stud partition wall or if you are cutting a new doorway you'll have to locate the vertical studs fairly accurately.

You might be able to do this simply by tapping the wall and listening for the dull thud that signifies something solid behind the plasterwork, but in practice this isn't always reliable and you need to drill a few test holes to locate the framework exactly.

In general, you can count on there being a stud at the edge of the partition where it meets another wall: measure from here to locate the next stud along, then drill a series of small holes to find its exact position. Studs are usually positioned at about 18in intervals so that wallboard covering can be fixed to them, but on older lath-and-plaster structures spacing can be unequal.

As a last resort, try cutting a small access hole in the cladding and use a length of stiff wire to find the stud, then gauge its position on the surface.

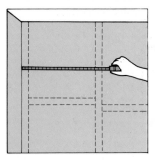
1. Measure 18in from the edge of the partition to find the next stud along

2. Tap the wall with a screwdriver near the pencil mark; listen for a dull sound

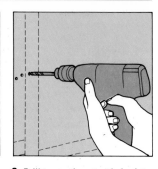
3. Drill two or three test holes into the wall until you see sawdust on the bit

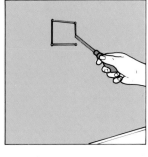
4. If you can't find the stud, cut a small access hole in the wall using a compass saw

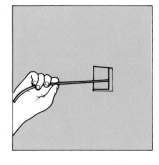
5. Straighten out an old wire coat hanger and feed one end into the access hole

6. If you meet an obstruction mark the wire's length with your thumb and transfer to the surface

Finding floor and ceiling joists

Where you're installing a stud partition wall – or you're making any other fixing to floor or ceiling – it is necessary to locate the exact position of the relevant joists to enable the structure to be fitted to them for strength and rigidity.

Joists are commonly 12, 14, 16 or 18in apart. In older properties such accuracy can't be relied on, though, and there may even be a mix of spacings.

Finding floor joists is quite straightforward if you can gain access to the floorboards: just look at the pattern of the nails. If the boards are covered with hardboard or something equally permanent, a glance at the floorboard direction in an adjoining room may save you from guessing.

The exact location of ceiling joists can be plotted by lifting the flooring in the room above or by looking at the 'floor' joists in the loft. Failing that, investigatory tapping and probing with a bradawl should pinpoint them.

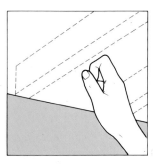
1. Tap the ceiling with your knuckles and listen for the dull thud over solid wood

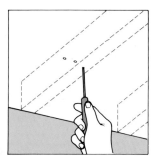
2. Poke a bradawl into the ceiling in this area until you locate the edges of the joist

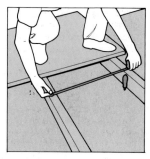
3. If possible push a bradawl through the attic floor and measure the joist spaces

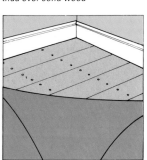
4. Lift the floorcovering to see the nail pattern – driven centrally into the joists

5. If the carpet is fitted, try looking in the adjoining room for the board nails

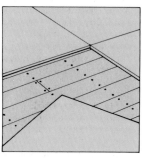
6. There may be no alternative to prying up a hardboard, floor tiles and so on

Hanging cabinets on walls

Convenient cabinet heights

When you're attaching cabinets to a wall, consider their positions for convenient use. Generally only long-term storage units should be over 6ft from the floor. Reserve the lowest shelves – no more than 4ft 6 in from the floor – for heavy, bulky or constantly-needed items so you don't have to stretch to reach them. The intermediate spaces can be for smaller items.

Choice of cabinet hangers

Although you can simply screw a cabinet to a wall, the range of hardware available offers adjustability, ease of fitting – and ease of removing the cabinet if need be. Choice is narrowed by holding capacities. Some KD (knock-down) fittings allow you to align the cabinet more accurately than is possible using screws alone. Two-part versions enable you to attach wall and cabinet fixings separately, making it easier to get the cabinet level.

1. *Position wall cabinets at a convenient height so you can reach all items inside easily*

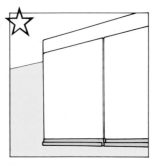

2. *If you run a cabinet up to an uneven ceiling at the top, fit a scribed molding strip*

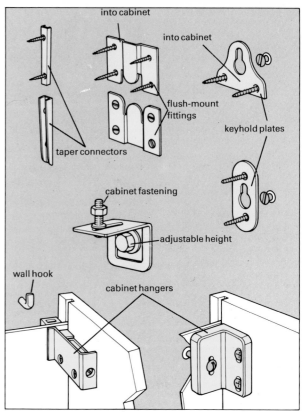

into cabinet
into cabinet
flush-mount fittings
keyhold plates
taper connectors
cabinet fastening
adjustable height
wall hook
cabinet hangers

Using bevelled hanging cleats

Although you can simply hang a cabinet on a series of wooden cleats, the result isn't always very neat.

One method that provides an inconspicuous fixing that's capable of supporting fairly heavy weights comprises a bevelled cleat which runs the width of the cabinet, just under the top panel. It's connected to the main carcase – bevel down – with dowels, glue and brads which also helps to strengthen the cabinet construction.

The cleat hooks over an identically-bevelled cleat – bevel uppermost – fixed to the wall with screws and wallplugs. These should be fairly stout No.10 screws. Your priority here is to insure the cleat is perfectly horizontal or the cabinet will be crooked (and cannot be adjusted). No other attachment is required, as the weight of the cabinet and its contents prevents the cleats from parting. This also means that the cabinet is extremely easy to remove from the wall if necessary.

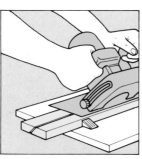

1. *Use a circular saw with angled sole plate to cut two cleats with 45° bevels*

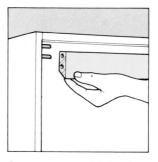

2. *Attach one end of the hanging cleat to one side of the cabinet with glued dowels*

3. *Attach the other side of the cabinet to the carcase, dowelling the hanging cleat*

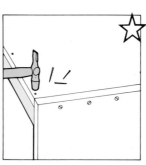

4. *Drive brads through the top panel into the hanging cleat for extra rigidity*

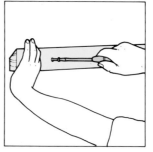

5. *Pre-drill the wall cleat, mark wall and fit plugs then screw cleat into place*

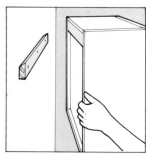

6. *Lift the cabinet against the wall and hook the bevelled cleat over its partner*

Attaching things to solid walls

Using wallplugs

Secure attachments to a solid wall are best made with screws instead of masonry nails (see below). Screws can't cut their own thread in masonry; plugs give the screw something to grip.

Traditional plugs are made of compressed wood fibers; they come in various sizes and lengths, with a central pilot hole. The hole and plug size must conform with the screw size.

Plastic plugs come in various sizes. As with fiber plugs, they must be matched to screw and hole.

Standard plastic wallplugs incorporate expanding fins and barbs, opening jaws or slits to increase the grip. One size will suffice for several screw sizes.

Buy plugs of the correct size for the screws: on plastered walls the screw should penetrate 1in into the masonry. For heavy fixings such as book-shelves, sink the screw 2in in the wall. The screw's shank shouldn't enter the plug.

When *drilling*, use a slow speed and withdraw the bit periodically to clear dust and allow the bit to cool. In very hard walls use a hammer-action drill.

Frame fixings. Window and door frames are screwed to the inside of the opening, but it's a difficult job to remove the frame.

Frame plugs allow you to drill through the frame into the masonry in one operation and insert the plug through the hole. Longer than wallplugs, they have a built-in screw (fig.6).

1. Don't drill attachment holes above switches, above or below lights or below sockets

2. A drill bit will wander on a surface such as tiles; use masking tape to prevent this

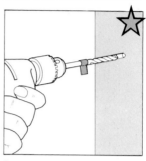

3. Wind adhesive tape round the drill bit the length of the screw from the tip, as a depth guide

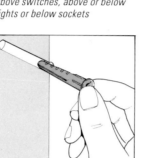

4. Push the plug into the hole so its wide rim is flush with the wall: tap in gently

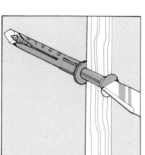

5. Hold the cleat (or other object) against the wall, insert the screw and drive home fully

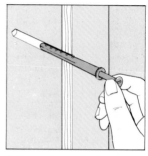

6. Insert a frame plug into the pre-drilled hole, then drive the screw in

7. In cinder block, drill a fairly large hole and hammer in a spiral-type finned plug

Fixings in soft walls

Standard wall fixings won't grip well in soft or crumbly masonry or in cinder block.

Use a special *cellular block plug* instead: it has flexible fins molded in a spiral to prevent the plug from rotating.

Another way to fix things to soft solid walls is to use a ready-mixed *resin-based filler*, especially useful if the wall is in bad condition and crumbly. It won't give a strong fixing but can be molded to shape.

To make a fixing, widen the hole at the back without broadening the mouth, so the filler will grip firmly. Pack it in well.

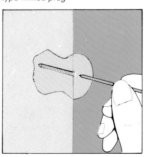

8. Press filler into the undercut hole, make a pilot hole, then drive in the screw

Using masonry nails

Primarily for hanging lightweight frame pictures, specially *hardened pins* (often with decorative heads where they're likely to be on show) usually come with metal picture hooks. They can be driven into most solid walls with a hammer (don't use a heavy hammer or you'll bend them).

The hooks dictate the downward angle in which the pin enters the wall, if you're using pins alone, angle them, too, so they won't pull out.

Masonry nails are extra-hard nails that are best suited to fixing shelving cleats, baseboards, or wall pannelling to brick, block, plastered and solid walls. Use them where appearance isn't important, but a permanent, strong fixing is.

There are two types, with a *plain shank* for general use; with a *twisted shank* for better penetration in dense walls.

Lengths range from 1in to 4in. Choose a nail that will penetrate the wall by at least 1in for a secure fixing.

Drive in masonry nails using a heavy *hammer* and hit the head heavily but squarely or there's a risk that it might bend or shatter: use multiple light taps rather than heavy hammer blows. *Wear goggles* to protect your eyes from flying debris.

If you're fixing up a wooden cleat drive in the nails so their points just break through on the opposite side, position the cleat, level it, then drive in the nails fully with multiple blows.

Insert the nails *dovetail fashion* – at an angle to the cleat – so there's less likelihood that they'll pull out of the wall.

1. To fit a cleat, dovetail masonry nails in so their points just break through the wood